Math: First Grade
Contents

Introduction	3
Correlation to NCTM Standards	4

Unit 1: Number Sense

Lesson 1: Numbers 0–10
Teacher Information	6
Writing and Modeling Numbers 1–10	8
Comparing Numbers 1–10	9
Matching Numbers and Words	10
Ordering Numbers	11
Solving Word Problems	12
Counting Colors	13
Clip Hunt	13

Lesson 2: Addition
Teacher Information	14
Understanding Addition	16
Writing Addition Sentences	17
Understanding Addition Order	18
Practicing Addition	19
Solving Word Problems	20
Showing 10	21
Number Riddles	21

Lesson 3: Subtraction
Teacher Information	22
Understanding Subtraction	24
Writing Subtraction Sentences	25
Practicing Subtraction	26
Practicing Subtraction	27
Solving Word Problems	28
What Will You Buy?	29
Find the Pattern	29

Lesson 4: Place Value: Numbers to 100
Teacher Information	30
Understanding Tens	32
Understanding Tens and Ones	33
Ordering Numbers	34
Ordering Numbers	35
Solving Word Problems	36
Birth Date Order	37
Favorite Number	37

Lesson 5: Addition and Subtraction to 18
Teacher Information	38
Using the Make a 10 Strategy	40
Practicing Addition and Subtraction	41
Writing Fact Families	42
Adding and Subtracting Numbers	43
Solving Word Problems	44
Writing Number Sentences	45
Adding Patterns	45

Unit 2: Algebra

Lesson 6: Patterns
Teacher Information	46
Identifying Patterns	48
Extending Color Patterns	49
Extending Size Patterns	50
Finding Patterns	51
Solving Word Problems	52
Coloring a Pattern	53
Making Pattern Pictures	53

Unit 3: Geometry

Lesson 7: Plane Figures
Teacher Information	54
Exploring Plane Figures	56
Classifying Plane Figures	57
Identifying Sides and Corners	58
Building with Plane Figures	59
Solving Word Problems	60
Making Eight	61
Looking for Six	61

Lesson 8: Solid Figures
Teacher Information	62
Exploring Solid Figures	64
Classifying Solid Figures	65
Understanding Solid Figures	66
Counting Solid Figures	67
Solving Word Problems	68
Counting Cubes	69
Learning About Solids	69

www.harcourtschoolsupply.com
© Harcourt Achieve Inc. All rights reserved.

Contents
Math: First Grade, SV 9937-6

Lesson 9: Symmetry
Teacher Information 70
Understanding Symmetry 72
Identifying Symmetry 73
Practicing Symmetry 74
Drawing Symmetrically 75
Solving Word Problems 76
Finding Letter Symmetry 77
Making Symmetry 77

Lesson 10: Fractions
Teacher Information 78
Understanding Fractions 80
Reading Fractions 81
Coloring Fractions 82
Finding Fractional Parts 83
Solving Word Problems 84
Naming a Pattern...85
Identifying Fraction Clocks 85

Unit 4: Measurement
Lesson 11: Length
Teacher Information 86
Understanding Measurement 88
Measuring with Inches 89
Measuring with Centimeters 90
Practicing Measurement..91
Solving Word Problems 92
Planning a Garden 93
Measuring a Desk 93

Lesson 12: Time
Teacher Information 94
Understanding Time to the Hour 96
Estimating Time...97
Writing Time to the Half Hour 98
Estimating Time to the Minute 99
Solving Word Problems 100
Baking Time...101
Going to Bed 101

Lesson 13: Money
Teacher Information 102
Identifying Coins 104
Counting Pennies and Nickels 105
Counting On 106
Counting Coins 107
Solving Word Problems 108
Trading Coins 109
Buying at a Bake Sale 109

Unit 5: Data and Analysis
Lesson 14: Graphs
Teacher Information 110
Understanding a Graph 112
Making a Graph 113
Reading a Graph 114
Practicing Graphing Skills 115
Solving Word Problems 116
Asking and Graphing 117
Making a Graph 117

Lesson 15: Probability
Teacher Information 118
Understanding Probability 120
Exploring Probability 121
Exploring Fair Games 122
Exploring Likely and Unlikely 123
Solving Word Problems 124
Choosing Shapes 125
Making a Game..125

Resources
Chart...126
Shapes 127
Clock 128

Introduction

The National Council of Teachers of Mathematics (NCTM) has targeted five content standards in an effort to help students reach their full potential as capable and mathematically competent individuals. The standards include Number and Operations, Algebra, Geometry, Measurement, and Data Analysis and Probability. Within the content standards, NCTM has listed topic standards and expectations for students at all grade levels. *Math* is a series that exposes students to many of the standards as they creatively explore new mathematic ideas and concepts.

Math targets the most important math topics for each grade level. Students gain exposure through hands-on experiences and then have an opportunity to build on this basic knowledge through practice and extension activities. Used as a supplement, *Math* can enhance the mathematical development of all students, no matter what their level of understanding.

Organization and Features

The book consists of five units that focus on the content standards. The 15 lessons in each book are proportional to the grade bands proposed by the NCTM. Each eight-page lesson consists of:

- **Teacher background and information**. A two-page introduction identifies the targeted standards, materials needed for the lesson, and a description of the activities. To help develop the concepts, the information page identifies **reteaching ideas**, **extension activities**, and suggestions that students can share with family members **at home**. Most importantly, the **answer key** is embedded in these pages to provide easier access between the activity pages and solutions. Finally, information is given about the **Harcourt Achieve website,** where other ideas are just a click away.

- **Manipulative component**. To introduce each concept, the first lesson page is devoted to the use of manipulatives so that students can explore important tenets in a concrete way.

- **Practice.** Follow-up practice is critical to help students transfer concrete understanding to the more abstract math concepts.

- **Extension**. This page allows students another page of practice, but in a more relaxed and inviting format. Students might answer riddles, draw pictures, or follow a code as they continue to practice skill development.

- **Word problems**. Students combine reading comprehension with mathematics as they utilize a variety of problem-solving techniques to answer relevant questions.

- **Enrichment**. The final page in each lesson outlines two open-ended activities that require more higher-level, logical, and creative thinking. They are self-directed and require materials available in the classroom.

In addition, each book contains:
- a table of contents that specifies each skill.
- a correlation chart that identifies the specific NCTM expectations by lesson.
- three resource pages to accompany activities.

What Research Says

"Research has solidly established the importance of conceptual understanding in becoming proficient in a subject. When students understand mathematics, they are able to use their knowledge flexibly. . . . Learning the 'basics' is important. . . . In contrast, conceptual understanding enables students to deal with novel problems and settings. They can solve problems that they have not encountered before."

Principles and Standards for School Mathematics: An Overview. 2000. Reston, VA: The National Council of Teachers of Mathematics, Inc.

Correlation to NCTM Standards

LESSONS

CONTENT STRANDS	1	2	3	4	5	6	7	8	9	10	11	12	13	14	15
Number and Operations															
• Count with understanding and recognize "how many" in sets of objects	•	•	•	•				•					•	•	
• Use multiple models to develop initial understandings of place value and the base-ten number system		•	•	•	•										
• Develop understanding of the relative position and magnitude of whole numbers and of ordinal and cardinal numbers and their connections	•														
• Develop a sense of whole numbers and represent and use them in flexible ways, including relating, composing, and decomposing numbers		•	•	•	•							•	•	•	
• Connect number words and numerals to the quantities they represent, using various physical models and representations		•	•	•	•								•		
• Understand various meanings of addition and subtraction of whole numbers and the relationship between the two operations		•	•												
• Understand the effects of adding and subtracting whole numbers		•	•		•										
• Use a variety of methods and tools to compute, including objects, mental computation, estimation, paper and pencil, and calculators															
• Understand and represent commonly used fractions, such as $\frac{1}{4}$, $\frac{1}{3}$, and $\frac{1}{2}$										•					
Algebra															
• Sort, classify, and order objects by size, number, and other properties						•	•	•	•						
• Recognize, describe, and extend patterns such as sequences of sounds and shapes or simple numeric patterns and translate from one representation to another		•				•									
• Analyze how both repeating and growing patterns are generated						•									

www.harcourtschoolsupply.com
© Harcourt Achieve Inc. All rights reserved.

Correlation Chart
Math: First Grade, SV 9937-6

Correlation to NCTM Standards

LESSONS

CONTENT STRANDS	1	2	3	4	5	6	7	8	9	10	11	12	13	14	15
Geometry															
• Recognize, name, build, draw, compare, and sort two- and three-dimensional shapes															
• Describe attributes and parts of two- and three-dimensional shapes							•	•	•						
• Investigate and predict the results of putting together and taking apart two- and three-dimensional shapes							•	•	•	•					
• Recognize and create shapes that have symmetry									•						
• Recognize and represent shapes from different perspectives							•	•	•	•					
• Recognize geometric shapes and structures in the environment and specify their location							•								
Measurement															
• Recognize the attributes of length, volume, weight, area, and time											•				
• Compare and order objects according to these attributes											•	•			
• Understand how to measure using nonstandard and standard units			•								•				
• Measure with multiple copies of units of the same size, such as paper clips laid end to end			•								•				
• Use tools to measure													•		
• Develop common referents for measures to make comparisons and estimates											•	•			
Data Analysis and Probability															
• Pose questions and gather data about themselves and their surroundings				•											
• Sort and classify objects according to their attributes and organize data about the objects											•			•	•
• Represent data using concrete objects, pictures, and graphs														•	•
• Describe parts of the data and the set of data as a whole to determine what the data show													•	•	•
• Discuss events related to students' experiences as likely or unlikely															•
Problem Solving															
• Apply and adapt a variety of appropriate strategies to solve problems		•	•	•					•	•		•	•		•

www.harcourtschoolsupply.com
© Harcourt Achieve Inc. All rights reserved.

Correlation Chart
Math: First Grade, SV 9937-6

Lesson 1

Numbers 0–10

Objectives

- Count with understanding and recognize "how many" in sets of objects
- Use multiple models to develop initial understandings of place value and the base-ten number system
- Develop understanding of the relative position and magnitude of whole numbers and of ordinal and cardinal numbers and their connections
- Develop a sense of whole numbers and represent and use them in flexible ways, including relating, composing, and decomposing numbers
- Connect number words and numerals to the quantities they represent, using various physical models and representations
- Understand how to measure using nonstandard and standard units
- Measure with multiple copies of units of the same size, such as paper clips laid end to end
- Apply and adapt a variety of appropriate strategies to solve problems

Materials

- pencils, beans, bi-colored counters, small bags, number cards 1–10, paper clips, construction paper (optional), stickers (optional), rhythm instruments (optional), craft paper (optional), dried lima beans (optional), self-sealing bags (optional)

Lesson Pages

Page 8 (Manipulatives)
Children trace a number and show the corresponding number of beans. Then they draw the beans.

Page 9 (Practice)
Children count groups of bugs and write the numbers. Then they circle the number that is greater.

Page 10 (Practice)
Children draw lines to match numerals to words.

Page 11 (Extension)
To help a lost clown find the circus, children draw lines to order numbers 0–10.

Page 12 (Word Problems)
Children solve word problems.

Page 13 (Enrichment)
Activity Card 1: Invite partners to count out 10 bi-colored counters and put them in a bag. Each child chooses a different color on the counter. Then they empty the bag 4 times. Children count the number of counters showing their color and record it in the chart each time. They circle to show the greater number.
Activity Card 2: Stack cards 1–10. Ask each child to choose a card and count out that number of paper clips. After placing the clips end to end, tell children to draw a paper-clip ruler that long. Challenge them to find 3 things that are about the same length and to draw a picture of them in the frames.

Another Look

- Write the numbers 0–10 at the top of separate sheets of construction paper. Place the corresponding number of stickers below the numbers. Have children finger-trace the number and place a counter on each sticker, counting out loud as they do so. (Visual, Kinesthetic, ELL)

- Pass out rhythm instruments. Call out a number from 1–10 or have children choose a number card. Have them tap their instruments to show the number. (Kinesthetic, Auditory, ELL)

Extension

- Write numbers 1–10 on sheets of construction paper. Pass them out to children. Invite those with cards to put themselves in order. Introduce ordinal numbers.

- Give groups of children a piece of craft paper. Have them draw a picture of a farm scene. Challenge them to include groups of 1–10 items in their picture.

At Home

- Use a permanent marker to color one side of dried lima beans. Have children count out 10 beans to put in self-sealing plastic bags. Send a bag home with each child. Suggest that they invite a family member to play the Counting Colors game on page 13. Ask children to return the bags for future use.

- Have children ask their parents for the coins that are in a pocket or wallet. Tell children to sort the coins and count each group.

- Visit www.harcourtachieve.com/achievementzone for additional ideas and activity pages.

Answer Key

Page 8
Children trace the numbers and draw the corresponding numbers of beans.

Page 9
1. 3, 1; Children circle 3.
2. 4, 8; Children circle 8.
3. 2, 5; Children circle 5.
4. 7, 9; Children circle 9.
5. 6, 4; Children circle 6.
6. 10, 8; Children circle 10.

Page 10
Children draw lines to correctly match the numbers and words.

Page 11
Children draw lines to order numbers 0–10.

Page 12
1. 3
2. Children color 7 birds.
3. 10
4. Children circle 4 nuts.

Page 13
Card 1: Answers will vary.
Card 2: Answers will vary.

Name _____ Date _____

WRITING AND MODELING NUMBERS 1-10

Bean Bowls

➡ **How many beans? Trace each number. Put that many beans in the bowl. Then draw the beans.**

www.harcourtschoolsupply.com
© Harcourt Achieve Inc. All rights reserved.

Lesson 1, Numbers 0–10: Manipulatives
Math: First Grade, SV 9937-6

Name _____ Date _____

COMPARING NUMBERS 1–10

Bugged About Numbers

➡ **Write how many. Then circle the number that is greater.**

1.

   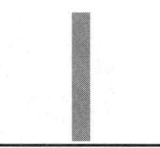

③   1
___   ___

2.

___   ___

3.

___   ___

4.

___   ___

5.

___   ___

6.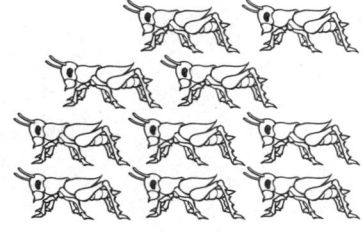

___   ___

www.harcourtschoolsupply.com
© Harcourt Achieve Inc. All rights reserved.

9

Lesson 1, Numbers 0–10: Practice
Math: First Grade, SV 9937-6

Name _____ Date _____

MATCHING NUMBERS AND WORDS
··

Words That Count

➡ **Draw lines to connect the numbers to their correct number words.**

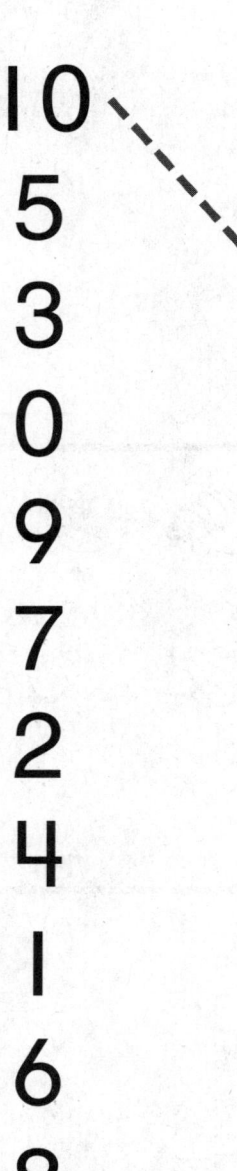

10	two
5	zero
3	six
0	three
9	five
7	eight
2	nine
4	ten
1	seven
6	four
8	one

www.harcourtschoolsupply.com
© Harcourt Achieve Inc. All rights reserved.

10

Lesson 1, Numbers 0–10: Practice
Math: First Grade, SV 9937-6

Name _____ Date _____

ORDERING NUMBERS
....

Go to the Circus

➡ **Help the clown go to the circus. Start with 0. Draw a line in order to 10.**

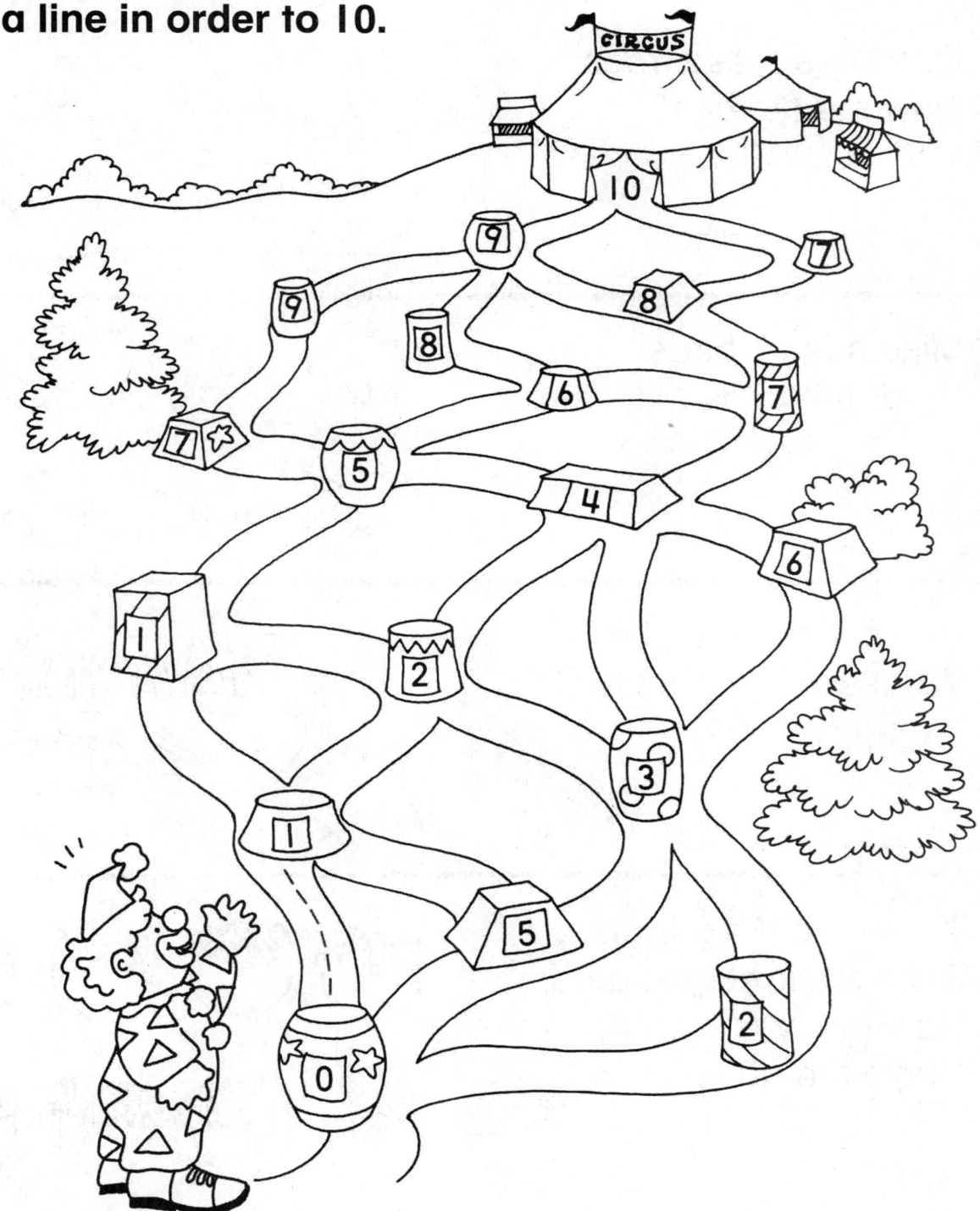

www.harcourtschoolsupply.com
© Harcourt Achieve Inc. All rights reserved.

Lesson 1, Numbers 0–10: Extension
Math: First Grade, SV 9937-6

Name _____ Date _____

SOLVING WORD PROBLEMS

On a Walk

 Read each story. Solve.

1. Rita sees these frogs.
How many frogs?

_____

2. Mike sees 7 birds.
Color the birds Mike sees.

3. Ben counts 9 ducks.
What will he count for
the next duck?

_____

4. There are 4 squirrels.
Each squirrel gets a nut.
How many nuts?
Circle the nuts.

www.harcourtschoolsupply.com
© Harcourt Achieve Inc. All rights reserved.

Lesson 1, Numbers 0–10: Word Problems
Math: First Grade, SV 9937-6

Name _____ Date _____

Counting Colors

➡ **Work with a friend. Choose a color on the counter. Put the counters in the bag. Let them fall out. How many of each color? Write the number. Circle the number that has more.**

	1	2	3	4
Name _____ Color _____				
Name _____ Color _____				

Name _____ Date _____

Clip Hunt

➡ **Choose a card. Write the number below. Put that many clips together. What is about that long? Draw 3 pictures.**

_____ clips

www.harcourtschoolsupply.com
© Harcourt Achieve Inc. All rights reserved.

Lesson 1, Numbers 0–10: Enrichment
Math: First Grade, SV 9937-6

Lesson 2

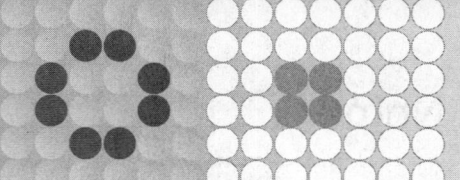

Addition

Objectives

- Count with understanding and recognize "how many" in sets of objects
- Use multiple models to develop initial understandings of place value and the base-ten number system
- Develop a sense of whole numbers and represent and use them in flexible ways, including relating, composing, and decomposing numbers
- Connect number words and numerals to the quantities they represent, using various physical models and representations
- Understand various meanings of addition and subtraction of whole numbers and the relationship between the two operations
- Understand the effects of adding and subtracting whole numbers
- Use a variety of methods and tools to compute, including objects, mental computation, estimation, paper and pencil, and calculators
- Recognize, describe, and extend patterns such as sequences of sounds and shapes or simple numeric patterns and translate from one representation to another
- Apply and adapt a variety of appropriate strategies to solve problems

Materials

- connecting cubes, pencils, crayons, masking tape (optional), permanent marker (optional), beanbags (optional), construction paper (optional), toys (optional), price tags (optional), pennies (optional), self-sealing plastic bags with bi-colored lima beans (optional)

Lesson Pages

Page 16 (Manipulatives)
Partners use two colors of connecting cubes to show groups. Then they join the cubes and write how many in all.

Page 17 (Practice)
Children count groups of animals that join together. Then they write the corresponding addition sentence.

Page 18 (Practice)
To develop an understanding of the commutative property of addition, children draw models and then draw lines to match sentences.

Page 19 (Extension)
After adding to find sums, children follow a code to color a picture.

Page 20 (Word Problems)
Children read addition stories and write the number sentences to solve them.

Page 21 (Enrichment)
Activity Card 1: Partners use two colors of connecting cubes to find and write ten addition sentences that make a sum of 10.
Activity Card 2: Children read and solve riddles about the addends in addition sentences.

Another Look

- As children complete the pages, encourage them to retell the stories by acting out the addition sentences. (Auditory, Kinesthetic, Visual, ELL)

- Make a tape number line 0–10 on the floor. Call out addition sentences and have children hop to the numbers to show the sum. (Visual, Kinesthetic, Auditory, ELL)

www.harcourtschoolsupply.com
© Harcourt Achieve Inc. All rights reserved.

Lesson 2, Addition: Teacher Information
Math: First Grade, SV 9937-6

Extension

- Write numbers 1–10 on separate pieces of construction paper. Lay them on the floor. Have children take turns tossing a beanbag on the numbers. Challenge them to say a number sentence having that sum.

- Gather some toys and label them with price tags to 10¢. Then give each child 10 pennies. Invite children to "shop" for the toys they would like to buy.

At Home

- Challenge children to use books and magazines to find pictures that they can use to make up addition stories to tell a family member.

- Send home the bags with 10 bi-colored lima beans. (See At Home on page 7.) Have children empty the bag and write the number sentence shown by the colors. Suggest they repeat the activity several times after removing several beans.

- Visit www.harcourtachieve.com/achievementzone for additional ideas and activity pages.

Answer Key

Page 16
1. 3
2. 5
3. 6
4. 6

Page 17
1. 3 + 1 = 4
2. 2 + 1 = 3
3. 5 + 1 = 6
4. 4 + 1 = 5

Page 18
For 1–2, children draw the correct number of *X*s.
1. 4, 4
2. 6, 6
For 3–6, children match the number sentences.
3. 5; 3 + 2 = 5
4. 5; 1 + 4 = 5
5. 9; 3 + 6 = 9
6. 9; 8 + 1 = 9
7. 7; 4 + 3 = 7
8. 8; 5 + 3 = 8

Page 19
Children find the sums and color the picture to match the code.

Page 20
1. 2 + 2 = 4
2. 6 + 3 = 9
3. 4 + 1 = 5
4. 3 + 5 = 8
5. 5 + 5 = 10

Page 21
Card 1: Answers will vary.
Card 2:
1. 5, 4
2. 3, 3
3. 4, 3
4. 5, 3

Name _____ Date _____

UNDERSTANDING ADDITION
....
Friendly Cubes

➡ **Work with a friend. Put cubes in box A. Have your friend put cubes in box B. Join the cubes. Write how many in all.**

1. | A ◻ ◻ | B ◻ | 3 |
   | Put in 2. | Put in 1 more. | in all |

2.  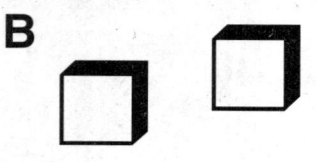 _____ in all

3. 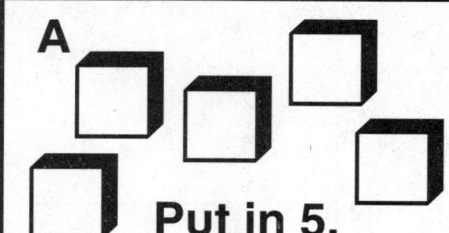 ◻ Put in 1 more. _____ in all

4.  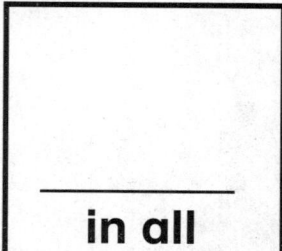 _____ in all

Box 3 A: Put in 5.   Box 3 B: Put in 1 more.
Box 4 A: Put in 4.   Box 4 B: Put in 2 more.

www.harcourtschoolsupply.com   16   Lesson 2, Addition: Manipulatives
© Harcourt Achieve Inc. All rights reserved.   Math: First Grade, SV 9937-6

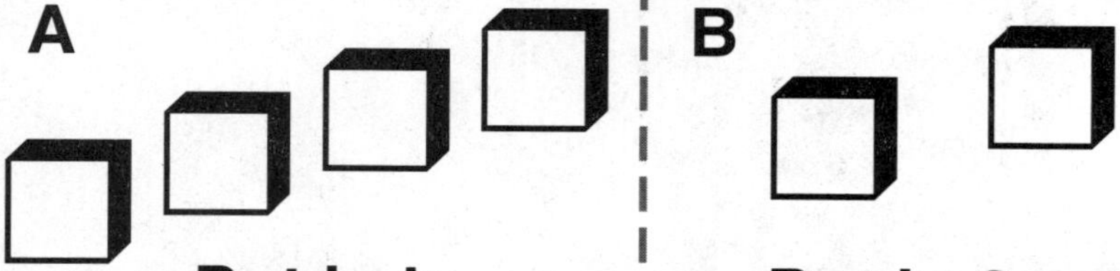

Name _____ Date _____

WRITING ADDITION SENTENCES
....

Join the Fun

▶ Write the addition sentence. Then write how many in all.

1.

   ___3___ + ___1___ = _____

2.

   _____ + _____ = _____

3.

   _____ + _____ = _____

4.

   _____ + _____ = _____

www.harcourtschoolsupply.com
© Harcourt Achieve Inc. All rights reserved.

17

Lesson 2, Addition: Practice
Math: First Grade, SV 9937-6

Name _____ Date _____

UNDERSTANDING ADDITION ORDER
••

Order Sorter

 Draw an **X** to show how many. Write the sum.

1.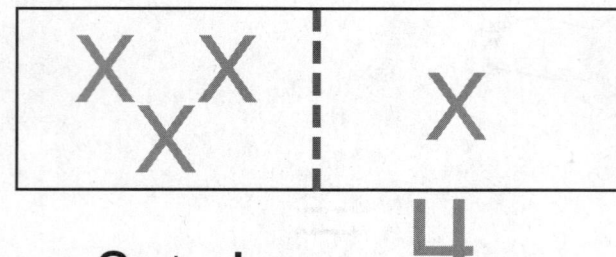

   3 + 1 = __4__   1 + 3 = __4__

2.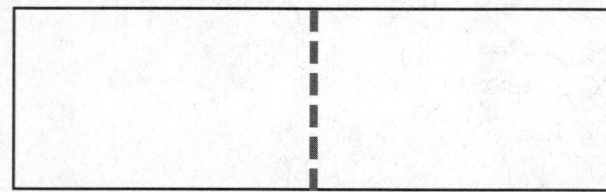

   2 + 4 = _____   4 + 2 = _____

 Add. Then match the addition sentences.

3. 2 + 3 = _____   1 + 4 = _____
4. 4 + 1 = _____   8 + 1 = _____
5. 6 + 3 = _____   3 + 2 = _____
6. 1 + 8 = _____   3 + 6 = _____
7. 3 + 4 = _____   5 + 3 = _____
8. 3 + 5 = _____   4 + 3 = _____

www.harcourtschoolsupply.com
© Harcourt Achieve Inc. All rights reserved.

18

Lesson 2, Addition: Practice
Math: First Grade, SV 9937-6

Name _____ Date _____

PRACTICING ADDITION

Up, Up, and Away

➡ Add. Then color the picture.

4–red   5–green   6–brown   7–yellow   8–blue

www.harcourtschoolsupply.com
© Harcourt Achieve Inc. All rights reserved.

Lesson 2, Addition: Extension
Math: First Grade, SV 9937-6

Name _____ Date _____

SOLVING WORD PROBLEMS
....
Park Play

➡ Read each story.
Write the addition sentence.

1. 2 girls are at the park.
2 girls run to the park.
How many girls in all? _____ + _____ = _____

2. 6 boys play ball.
3 boys fly a kite.
How many boys in all? _____ + _____ = _____

3. 4 dogs run.
1 dog sits.
How many dogs in all? _____ + _____ = _____

4. 3 tables with people.
5 tables with no people.
How many tables in all? _____ + _____ = _____

5. 5 girls swing.
5 boys slide.
How many children in all? _____ + _____ = _____

www.harcourtschoolsupply.com
© Harcourt Achieve Inc. All rights reserved.

20

Lesson 2, Addition: Word Problems
Math: First Grade, SV 9937-6

Name _____ Date _____

Showing 10

➤ Get 10 red cubes. Have a friend get 10 yellow cubes. How many ways can you show 10? Write 10 number sentences.

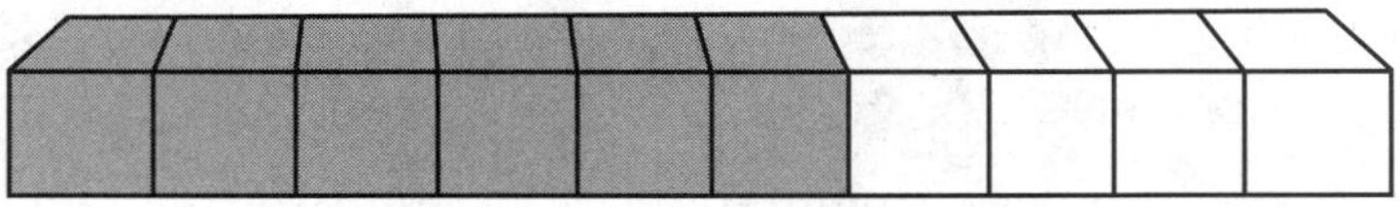

6 + 4 = 10

____ + ____ = ____   ____ + ____ = ____
____ + ____ = ____   ____ + ____ = ____
____ + ____ = ____   ____ + ____ = ____
____ + ____ = ____   ____ + ____ = ____
____ + ____ = ____   ____ + ____ = ____

Name _____ Date _____

Number Riddles

➤ Read each riddle. Find the numbers.

1. The sum is 9.
   The difference is 1.
   Both numbers are less than 6.
   What are the numbers?

   _____ and _____

2. The sum is 6.
   The difference is 0.
   What are the numbers?

   _____ and _____

3. The sum is 2 more than 5.
   The difference is 1 less than 2.
   What are the numbers?

   _____ and _____

4. The sum is 1 more than 7.
   The difference is 2 less than 4.
   What are the numbers?

   _____ and _____

www.harcourtschoolsupply.com
© Harcourt Achieve Inc. All rights reserved.

21

Lesson 2, Addition: Enrichment
Math: First Grade, SV 9937-6

Lesson 3

Subtraction

Objectives

- Count with understanding and recognize "how many" in sets of objects
- Use multiple models to develop initial understandings of place value and the base-ten number system
- Develop a sense of whole numbers and represent and use them in flexible ways, including relating, composing, and decomposing numbers
- Connect number words and numerals to the quantities they represent, using various physical models and representations
- Understand various meanings of addition and subtraction of whole numbers and the relationship between the two operations
- Understand the effects of adding and subtracting whole numbers
- Use a variety of methods and tools to compute, including objects, mental computation, estimation, paper and pencil, and calculators
- Recognize, describe, and extend patterns such as sequences of sounds and shapes or simple numeric patterns and translate from one representation to another
- Apply and adapt a variety of appropriate strategies to solve problems

Materials

- connecting cubes, pencils, crayons, masking tape (optional), permanent marker (optional), sheet (optional), index cards (optional), plastic cups (optional), construction paper cards (optional)

Lesson Pages

Page 24 (Manipulatives)
Partners use connecting cubes to show groups. Then they take away some cubes and write how many are left.

Page 25 (Practice)
Children count groups of birds and cross out the ones that are leaving. Then they write the corresponding subtraction sentence.

Page 26 (Practice)
Children complete subtraction sentences.

Page 27 (Extension)
After subtracting to find differences, children follow a code to color a picture.

Page 28 (Word Problems)
Children read subtraction stories and write the number sentences to solve them.

Page 29 (Enrichment)
Activity Card 1: Children make at least 3 lists of items they can buy with 10¢.
Activity Card 2: In this activity, children look for the subtraction pattern formed by connecting cube trains. Then they make their own cube models to show a different subtracting pattern for a partner to identify.

Another Look

- Make a tape number line that goes to 10 on the floor. Call out subtraction sentences. Invite children to hop along the number line to find the answer. (Visual, Kinesthetic, Auditory, ELL)

www.harcourtschoolsupply.com
© Harcourt Achieve Inc. All rights reserved.

22

Lesson 3, Subtraction: Teacher Information
Math: First Grade, SV 9937-6

- Review the song "Ten in the Bed." Then lay a sheet on the floor. Have children pantomime the action as they sing. Then help children figure out the corresponding subtraction sentence. You may do a song innovation in which more than one child "falls" out of bed. (Kinesthetic, Visual)

Extension

- On index cards, write 10 pairs of subtraction sentences that have the same difference, but do not write the answers. Invite children to play Concentration with the cards.

- Using two colors of cubes, put up to 10 cubes in plastic cups. Have children write 2 subtraction sentences that can name each cup.

At Home

- Ask children to tell subtraction stories to family members. Suggest that they look for actions and events that they can use in their stories. Ask children to draw a favorite story to share with the class the following day.

- Cut paper into small cards. Each child will need 13. Have children write 0–10, a minus sign, and an equals sign on the cards. Ask them to take the cards home and make true subtraction sentences to show family members.

- Visit www.harcourtachieve.com/achievementzone for additional ideas and activity pages.

Answer Key

Page 24
1. 2
2. 3
3. 5
4. 4

Page 25
1. 4 − 1 = 3
2. 6 − 1 = 5
3. 3 − 1 = 2
4. 4 − 2 = 2

Page 26
1. 1
2. 2
3. 4
4. 4
5. 2
6. 4

Page 27
Children find the differences and color the picture to match the code.

Page 28
1. 6 − 3 = 3
2. 8 − 4 = 4
3. 10 − 3 = 7
4. 3 − 3 = 0
5. 5 − 2 = 3

Page 29
Card 1: Answers will vary.
Card 2: The pattern is take away 2.

Name _____ Date _____

UNDERSTANDING SUBTRACTION
....

Take Away Cubes

➡ **Work with a friend. Put cubes in the box. Have your friend take away cubes by marking them with an X. Then write how many are left.**

1. [▢ ▢ ⊠]   __2__ are left.
Put in 3.
Take away 1.

2. [▢ ▢ ▢ ▢ ▢]   ____ are left.
Put in 5.
Take away 2.

3. [▢ ▢ ▢ ▢ / ▢ ▢ ▢ ▢]   ____ are left.
Put in 8.
Take away 3.

4. [▢ ▢ ▢ ▢ ▢ / ▢ ▢ ▢ ▢ ▢]   ____ are left.
Put in 10.
Take away 6.

www.harcourtschoolsupply.com
© Harcourt Achieve Inc. All rights reserved.

24

Lesson 3, Subtraction: Manipulatives
Math: First Grade, SV 9937-6

Name _____ Date _____

WRITING SUBTRACTION SENTENCES
··

Bye, Bye, Bird

➥ **Cross out the bird that is going away. Write the subtraction sentence. Then write how many are left.**

1.

4 — 1 = ___

2.

___ — ___ = ___

3.

___ — ___ = ___

4.

___ — ___ = ___

Name _____ Date _____

PRACTICING SUBTRACTION
....
Animal Take Away

 Cross out to subtract. Write the difference.

1.

3 − 2 = _____

2.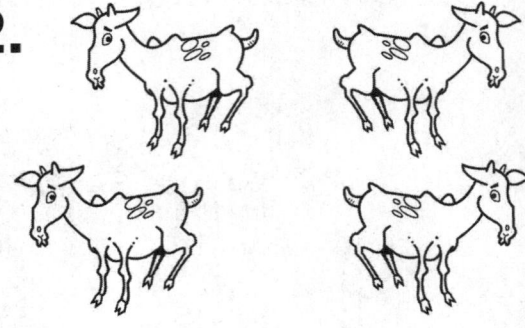

4 − 2 = _____

3.

5 − 1 = _____

4.

7 − 3 = _____

5.

5 − 3 = _____

6.

8 − 4 = _____

www.harcourtschoolsupply.com
© Harcourt Achieve Inc. All rights reserved.

26

Lesson 3, Subtraction: Practice
Math: First Grade, SV 9937-6

Name _____   Date _____

PRACTICING SUBTRACTION
··

Picture This

➡ **Subtract. Then color the picture.**

3–blue**4–green****5–red****6–brown****7–yellow**

$\begin{array}{r}8\\-5\\\hline\end{array}$ $\begin{array}{r}7\\-4\\\hline\end{array}$ $\begin{array}{r}6\\-3\\\hline\end{array}$ $\begin{array}{r}10\\-3\\\hline\end{array}$

$\begin{array}{r}9\\-4\\\hline\end{array}$ $\begin{array}{r}8\\-3\\\hline\end{array}$ $\begin{array}{r}4\\-1\\\hline\end{array}$

$\begin{array}{r}7\\-2\\\hline\end{array}$

$\begin{array}{r}9\\-6\\\hline\end{array}$ $\begin{array}{r}6\\-1\\\hline\end{array}$ $\begin{array}{r}10\\-5\\\hline\end{array}$ $\begin{array}{r}3\\-0\\\hline\end{array}$ $\begin{array}{r}5\\-2\\\hline\end{array}$

$\begin{array}{r}9\\-5\\\hline\end{array}$ $\begin{array}{r}6\\-2\\\hline\end{array}$ $\begin{array}{r}7\\-1\\\hline\end{array}$

$\begin{array}{r}4\\-0\\\hline\end{array}$

$\begin{array}{r}9\\-3\\\hline\end{array}$ $\begin{array}{r}8\\-2\\\hline\end{array}$ $\begin{array}{r}10\\-4\\\hline\end{array}$ $\begin{array}{r}6\\-0\\\hline\end{array}$

$\begin{array}{r}8\\-4\\\hline\end{array}$ $\begin{array}{r}10\\-6\\\hline\end{array}$ $\begin{array}{r}7\\-3\\\hline\end{array}$ $\begin{array}{r}5\\-1\\\hline\end{array}$

www.harcourtschoolsupply.com
© Harcourt Achieve Inc. All rights reserved.

Lesson 3, Subtraction: Extension
Math: First Grade, SV 9937-6

Name _____ Date _____

SOLVING WORD PROBLEMS

Along the Beach

➡ Read each story. Write the subtraction sentence.

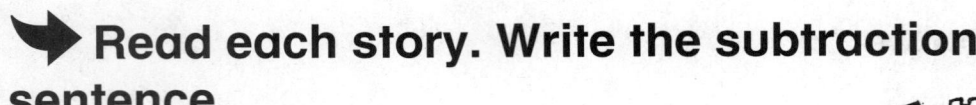

1. Rob finds 6 🐚. 
   He gives 3 away.
   How many are left?   _____ − _____ = _____

2. Tran sees 8 🦀. 
   4 run away.
   How many are left?   _____ − _____ = _____

3. Deb sees 10 🐟. 
   3 swim away.
   How many are left?   _____ − _____ = _____

4. Maria has 3 ⚽. 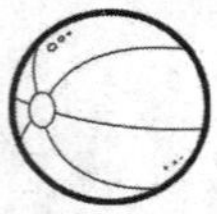
   3 balls roll away.
   How many are left?   _____ − _____ = _____

5. Lee makes 5 🏰. 
   2 break.
   How many are left?   _____ − _____ = _____

www.harcourtschoolsupply.com
© Harcourt Achieve Inc. All rights reserved.

Lesson 3, Subtraction: Word Problems
Math: First Grade, SV 9937-6

Name _____ Date _____

What Will You Buy?

➤ You have 10¢. What can you buy? Make 3 lists on another paper.

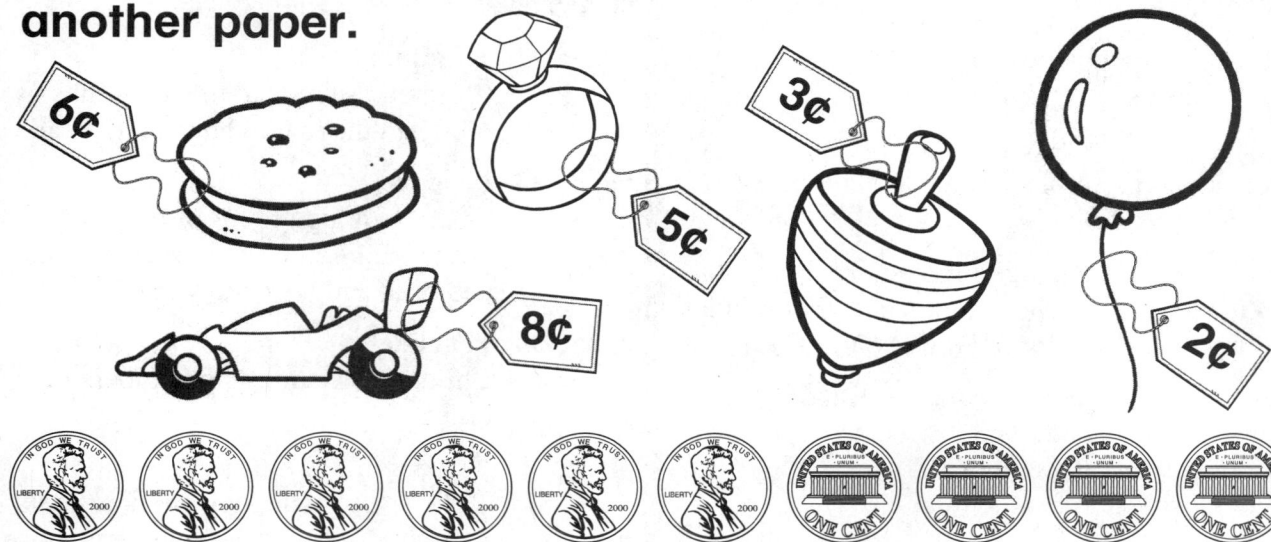

Name _____ Date _____

Find the Pattern

➤ What pattern do you see? Write the number sentences. Then use cubes to make your own pattern.

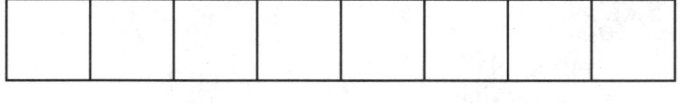

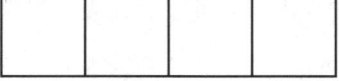
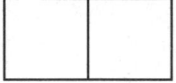

www.harcourtschoolsupply.com

© Harcourt Achieve Inc. All rights reserved.

Lesson 3, Subtraction: Enrichment
Math: First Grade, SV 9937-6

Lesson 4

Place Value: Numbers to 100

 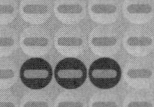 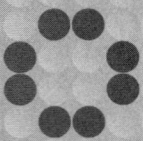 

Objectives

- Count with understanding and recognize "how many" in sets of objects
- Use multiple models to develop initial understandings of place value and the base-ten number system
- Develop understanding of the relative position and magnitude of whole numbers and of ordinal and cardinal numbers and their connections
- Develop a sense of whole numbers and represent and use them in flexible ways, including relating, composing, and decomposing numbers
- Connect number words and numerals to the quantities they represent, using various physical models and representations
- Pose questions and gather data about themselves and their surroundings
- Apply and adapt a variety of appropriate strategies to solve problems

Materials

- rods, cubes, pencils, boxes or baskets (optional), connecting cubes (optional), craft paper (optional), permanent marker (optional), 100 Chart blackline on page 126 (optional), bean bag (optional), number cards (optional), construction paper (optional), scissors (optional), hole punches (optional), self-sealing plastic bags (optional)

Lesson Pages

Page 32 Manipulatives
Children use rods to model groups of 10. Then they write how many in all.

Page 33 Practice
After counting groups of rods and cubes, children write how many tens and ones and how many in all.

Page 34 Practice
Children write missing numbers in order.

Page 35 Extension
To help the groundhog get back to its burrow, children color numbered boxes that increase in value to show a path.

Page 36 Word Problems
Children read stories and solve problems about books.

Page 37 Enrichment
Activity Card 1: Children take a poll of birth dates and record the answers on a chart. Then they order the dates.
Activity Card 2: Children try to figure out Josie's favorite number from clues. The clues narrow the choices to four numbers. Children write the last clue.

Another Look

- Gather several containers and number them. Then place handfuls of connecting cubes in each container. Have children make trains of 10 cubes to find how many are in each and record the number. Remind children to pull apart the cubes and replace them in the correct container when they are done. (Kinesthetic, Visual, ELL)

- On craft paper, make a 100 chart. Have children toss a beanbag on the chart, name the number, and model it with connecting cubes. (Visual, Kinesthetic, ELL)

Extension

- Use the chart on page 126. Choose a skill to work on, such as missing numbers, skip counting, or number patterns. Fill in the chart appropriately and make copies. Then have children complete the activity.

- Give each child number cards 0–9. Pair children and ask them to turn their cards facedown. Have each child select the top card and turn it faceup. Have partners form the greatest number.

At Home

- Cut 1-inch x 4-inch strips of construction paper. Give each child 10 strips and have the students punch 10 holes in each. After putting the strips in self-sealing plastic bags, ask children to take the strips home and count by tens for family members.

- Remind children that they have 10 fingers. Then ask children to draw a picture of the people living in their house. Suggest that they show the picture to a family member and count by tens to tell how many fingers are there.

- Visit www.harcourtachieve.com/achievementzone for additional ideas and activity pages.

Answer Key

Page 32
1. 20
2. 30
3. 50
4. 70

Page 33
1. 1, 4, 14
2. 1, 8, 18
3. 2, 2, 22
4. 4, 6, 46
5. 9, 9, 99

Page 34
1. 62, 63, 64, 66, 68, 69, 70
2. 58, 59, 60, 62, 63, 64, 65
3. 21, 22, 25, 26, 27, 28, 29
4. 47, 48, 49, 51, 52, 53
5. 90, 91, 93, 94, 96, 98
6. 70, 71, 74, 75, 76, 78, 79

Page 35
The path is: 12, 13, 17, 21, 25, 26, 32, 37, 43, 44, 47, 52, 64, 69, 75, 80, 84, 89, 92, 96, 99.

Page 36
1. 55
2. 70
3. Sally
4. 46, 47, 50

Page 37
Card 1: Answers will vary.
Card 2: Possible numbers for the given clues: 38, 56, 74, 92. The final clue and number will vary.

Name _____ Date _____

UNDERSTANDING TENS
··

We're a Group

➡ **Use rods. Show how many groups. Draw pictures. Write how many in all.**

1.
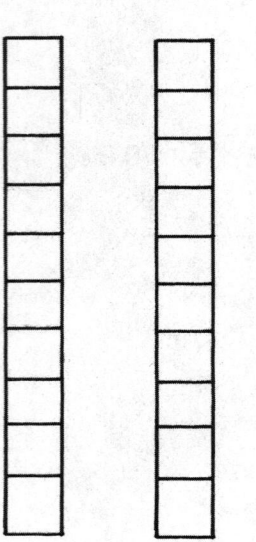
2 groups of 10 __20__

2.

3 groups of 10 _____

3.

5 groups of 10 _____

4.

7 groups of 10 _____

www.harcourtschoolsupply.com
© Harcourt Achieve Inc. All rights reserved.

32

Lesson 4, Place Value: Manipulatives
Math: First Grade, SV 9937-6

Name _____ Date _____

UNDERSTANDING TENS AND ONES

Building Blocks

➡ Write how many tens. Write how many ones. Write how many in all.

1. ▭▭▭▭▭▭▭▭▭▭ ▭ ▭ ▭ ▭

_____ ten _____ ones _____

2. ▭▭▭▭▭▭▭▭▭▭ ▭ ▭ ▭ ▭ ▭ ▭ ▭

_____ ten _____ ones _____

3. ▭▭▭▭▭▭▭▭▭▭ ▭▭▭▭▭▭▭▭▭▭ ▭ ▭

_____ tens _____ ones _____

4. ▭▭▭▭▭▭▭▭▭▭ ▭▭▭▭▭▭▭▭▭▭ ▭▭▭▭▭▭▭▭▭▭ ▭▭▭▭▭▭▭▭▭▭
   ▭ ▭ ▭ ▭ ▭

_____ tens _____ ones _____

5. ▭▭▭▭▭▭▭▭▭▭ ▭▭▭▭▭▭▭▭▭▭ ▭▭▭▭▭▭▭▭▭▭ ▭▭▭▭▭▭▭▭▭▭
   ▭▭▭▭▭▭▭▭▭▭ ▭▭▭▭▭▭▭▭▭▭ ▭▭▭▭▭▭▭▭▭▭ ▭▭▭▭▭▭▭▭▭▭
   ▭▭▭▭▭▭▭▭▭▭ ▭ ▭ ▭ ▭ ▭ ▭ ▭ ▭

_____ tens _____ ones _____

www.harcourtschoolsupply.com
© Harcourt Achieve Inc. All rights reserved.

Lesson 4, Place Value: Practice
Math: First Grade, SV 9937-6

Name _____ Date _____

ORDERING NUMBERS

Puzzled by Numbers

➡ Write the missing numbers.

1.  61 ___ ___ ___ 65 ___ 67 ___ ___ ___

2.  56 57 ___ ___ 61 ___ ___ ___

3. 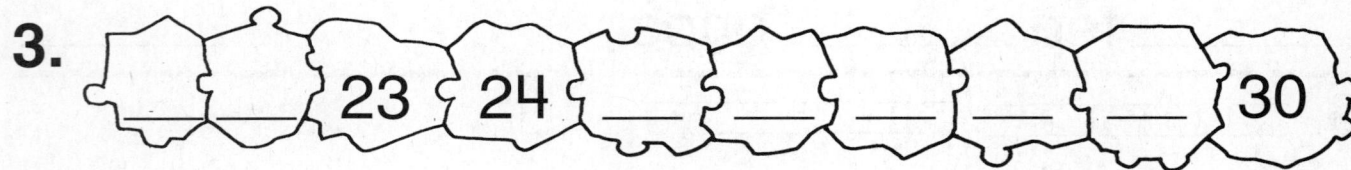 ___ 23 24 ___ ___ ___ ___ ___ 30

4.  45 46 ___ ___ ___ 50 ___ ___ ___ 54

5. 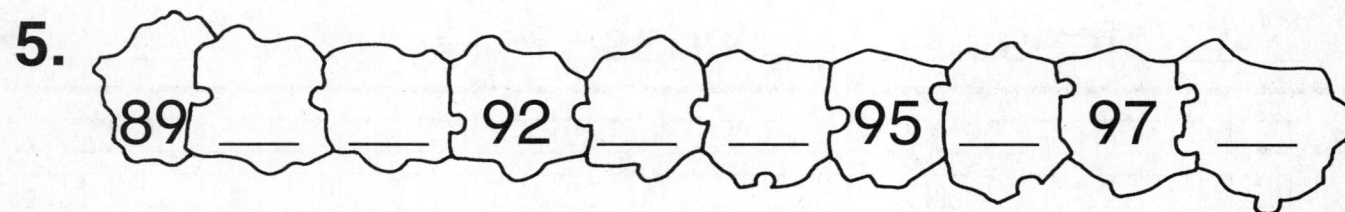 89 ___ ___ 92 ___ ___ 95 ___ 97 ___

6. 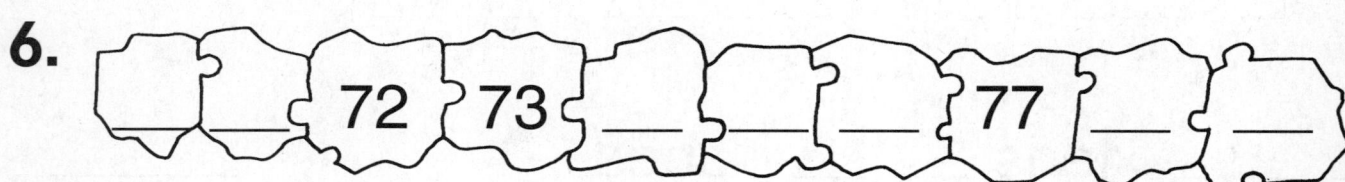 ___ 72 73 ___ ___ ___ ___ 77 ___

www.harcourtschoolsupply.com

© Harcourt Achieve Inc. All rights reserved.

34

Lesson 4, Place Value: Practice
Math: First Grade, SV 9937-6

Name _____ Date _____

ORDERING NUMBERS
•••
Number Path

➤ Help the groundhog get home. Color the boxes to make a path. Start at 12. Go to a higher number each time.

12	8	2	56	24	87	99
10	13	9	16	35	96	88
6	17	11	18	71	92	42
15	10	21	4	89	13	37
12	16	25	1	84	76	68
7	22	26	15	80	62	45
18	32	20	19	63	75	58
37	25	28	40	23	41	69
31	43	44	47	52	64	45

www.harcourtschoolsupply.com
© Harcourt Achieve Inc. All rights reserved.

35

Lesson 4, Place Value: Extension
Math: First Grade, SV 9937-6

Name _____ Date _____

SOLVING WORD PROBLEMS
....

The Problems with Books

➡ **Read each story. Solve.**

1. The library checked out these books one day. Write how many.

   _____ books

2. There are 10 books on each shelf. There are 7 shelves. Write how many books.

   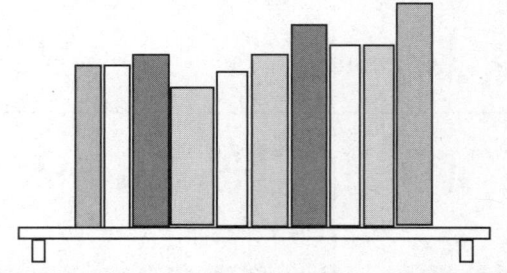

   _____ books

3. Sally gets a book with 32 pages. Lee gets a book with 23 pages. Who has more pages to read? Circle the name.

   Sally   Lee

4. Rosa is reading a book. Some pages are missing. Write the missing page numbers.

   | 45 | ___ | ___ | 48 | 49 | ___ | 51 |

Name _____ Date _____

Birth Date Order

➡ **Write your name on the chart. Write the day of the month on which you were born beside your name. Write the name and the birth date of 4 more people. Then write the days in number order under the chart.**

Name	Birth Date
_____	_____
_____	_____
_____	_____
_____	_____
_____	_____

____ ____ ____ ____ ____

Name _____ Date _____

Favorite Number

➡ **Josie has a favorite number.**

- It is an even number.
- It has 2 digits.
- Its digits equal 11.

How many numbers fit all the clues? Write them.

_____ _____ _____ _____ _____

Write 1 more clue. Give the clue to a friend. Ask the friend to guess the number.

_____

www.harcourtschoolsupply.com
© Harcourt Achieve Inc. All rights reserved.

Lesson 4, Place Value: Enrichment
Math: First Grade, SV 9937-6

Lesson 5

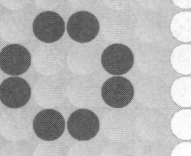

Addition and Subtraction to 18

Objectives

- Count with understanding and recognize "how many" in sets of objects
- Use multiple models to develop initial understandings of place value and the base-ten number system
- Develop a sense of whole numbers and represent and use them in flexible ways, including relating, composing, and decomposing numbers
- Connect number words and numerals to the quantities they represent, using various physical models and representations
- Understand various meanings of addition and subtraction of whole numbers and the relationship between the two operations
- Understand the effects of adding and subtracting whole numbers
- Use a variety of methods and tools to compute, including objects, mental computation, estimation, paper and pencil, and calculators
- Recognize, describe, and extend patterns such as sequences of sounds and shapes or simple numeric patterns and translate from one representation to another
- Apply and adapt a variety of appropriate strategies to solve problems

Materials

- counters, pencils, 3 colors of connecting cubes, construction paper (optional), number cubes (optional), scrap paper (optional), index cards (optional), music tape or CD (optional), tape player or CD player (optional), self-sealing plastic bag with bi-colored lima beans (optional)

Lesson Pages

Page 40 (Manipulatives)
Children use a 10-frame and counters to practice adding using the make a 10 strategy. Then they write the sums.

Page 41 (Practice)
Using the Commutative Property of Addition, children practice writing and solving addition and subtraction sentences.

Page 42 (Practice)
Children find the number sentences in fact families.

Page 43 (Extension)
Children find the missing numbers in algorithms to solve a riddle.

Page 44 (Word Problems)
Children read stories about puppies and solve them using either addition or subtraction.

Page 45 (Enrichment)
Activity Card 1: Children write number sentences using given numbers as the sums or differences.
Activity Card 2: Children use 18 connecting cubes in 3 different colors to create a pattern. Then they write the addition sentence to show the number of cubes.

Another Look

- Give partners 9 each of blue and red connecting cubes. Call out a number from 10 to 18. Have one child use some red and some blue cubes to make a cube train. Challenge the partner to say 2 addition and 2 subtraction sentences to show the fact family. Then have partners switch roles to show the same number. (Visual, Kinesthetic, Auditory, ELL)

www.harcourtschoolsupply.com
© Harcourt Achieve Inc. All rights reserved.

Lesson 5, Addition and Subtraction to 18: Teacher Information
Math: First Grade, SV 9937-6

- Write numbers 1–18 on separate sheets of construction paper. Make a number line with the numbers. Then give groups of three children a number cube. Have two players take turns rolling a cube, saying the corresponding number sentence, and moving that many spaces along the number line. The third child writes the addition sentence each time. When the children reach 18, they return using subtraction sentences. Have the players and recorders switch places. (Visual, Kinesthetic, Auditory, ELL)

Extension

- Give each child an index card and ask children to write a number from 1–9. Then divide children into 2 groups. Have them form two circles, one inside the other. Then play an innovation of musical chairs. While the music plays, the inner circle walks clockwise, and the outer circle walks counterclockwise. When the music stops, children pair up with someone who is in the other circle and say the addition fact using their numbers.

- Challenge children to use the activity above to practice subtraction sentences. Make numbers from 1–18. Pass out numbers 1–9 to children in the inner circle. Pass out numbers 10–18 to children in the outer circle. Partners from the two circles say the subtraction sentence when the music stops.

At Home

- Tell children to find a wall calendar and a marker, like a coin. Ask them to have a family member put the coin on a date and ask children to add up to 3 more or subtract 3 or fewer.

- Send home bags with 18 bi-colored lima beans. (See At Home on page 7.) Have children empty the bag and write the fact family sentences shown by the colors. Suggest they repeat the activity several times after removing several beans.

- Visit www.harcourtachieve.com/achievementzone for additional ideas and activity pages.

Answer Key

Page 40
1. 11; 14; 12; 14
2. 15; 11; 12; 11
3. 14; 13; 16; 17

Page 41
1. 7, 7 + 5 = 12; 5, 5 + 9 = 14; 8, 8 + 8 = 16
2. 5; 5 + 6 = 11; 5, 5 + 8 = 13; 8, 8 + 9 = 17
3. 8, 8 + 7 = 15; 9, 9 + 9 = 18; 7, 7 + 4 = 11

Page 42
1. 6 + 7 = 13   7 + 6 = 13
   13 − 7 = 6   13 − 6 = 7
2. 6 + 9 = 15   9 + 6 = 15
   15 − 6 = 9   15 − 9 = 6
3. 8 + 4 = 12   4 + 8 = 12
   12 − 8 = 4   12 − 4 = 8
4. 6 + 5 = 11   5 + 6 = 11
   11 − 6 = 5   11 − 5 = 6
5. 9 + 8 = 17   8 + 9 = 17
   17 − 9 = 8   17 − 8 = 9

Page 43
B-12
N-7
Y-6
A-8
R-11
E-14
Riddle: Barney

Page 44
1. 14 − 5 = 9
2. 6 + 7 = 13
3. 3 + 8 = 11
4. 17 − 8 = 9

Page 45
Card 1: Answers will vary.
Card 2: Answers will vary.

Name _____ Date _____

USING THE MAKE A 10 STRATEGY

Picture This Frame

➡ **Use counters and the 10-frame. Start with the greater number. Make a 10. Then add.**

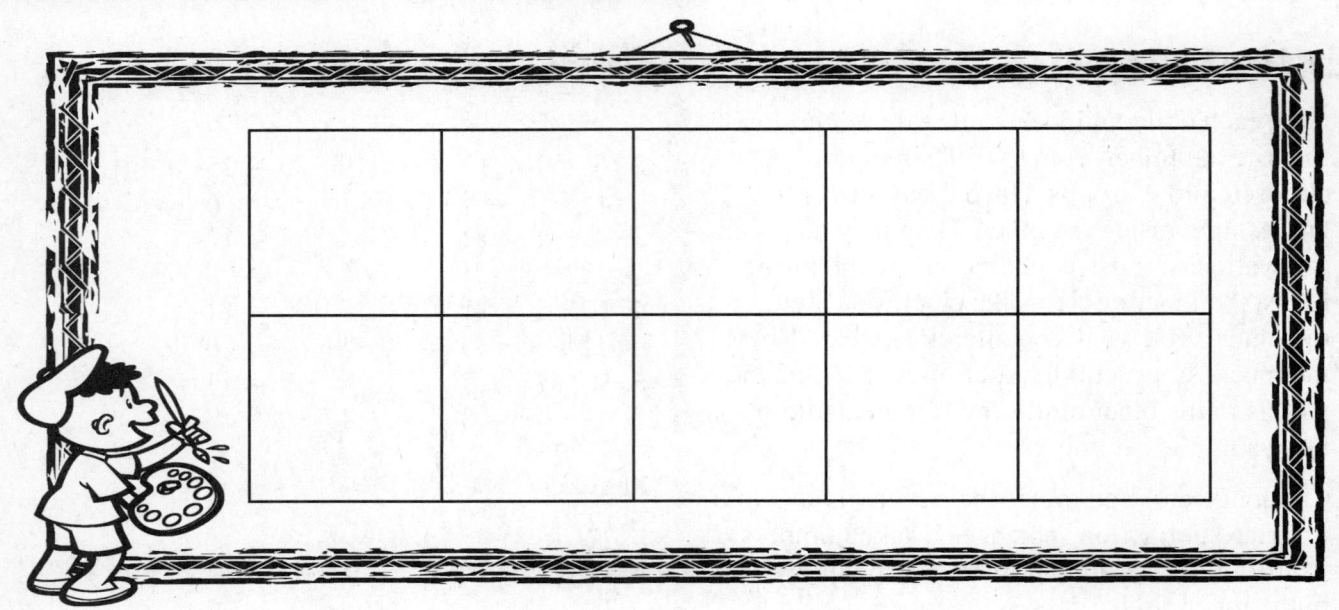

1.   7   8   3   6
   +4   +6   +9   +8

2.   9   3   7   2
   +6   +8   +5   +9

3.   5   4   7   8
   +9   +9   +9   +9

www.harcourtschoolsupply.com   Lesson 5, Addition and Subtraction to 18: Manipulatives
© Harcourt Achieve Inc. All rights reserved.   Math: First Grade, SV 9937-6

Name _____ Date _____

PRACTICING ADDITION AND SUBTRACTION

Mitten Match

▶ Write the addition facts that help. Then complete the subtraction facts.

1.

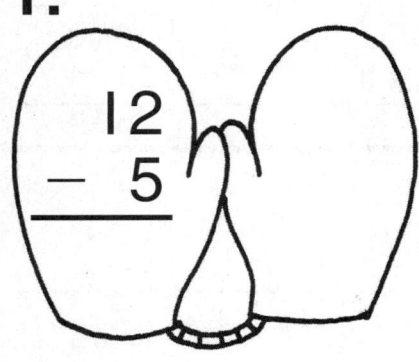

12 − 5

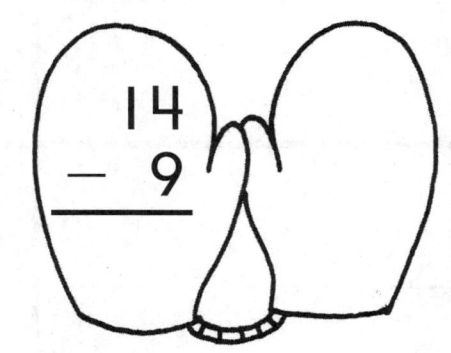

14 − 9

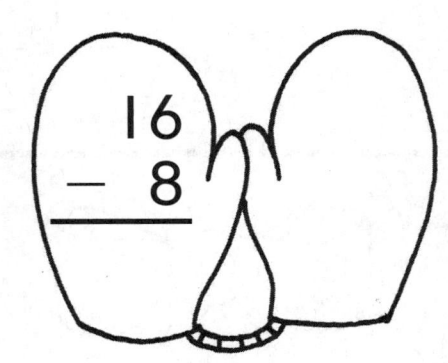

16 − 8

2.

11 − 6

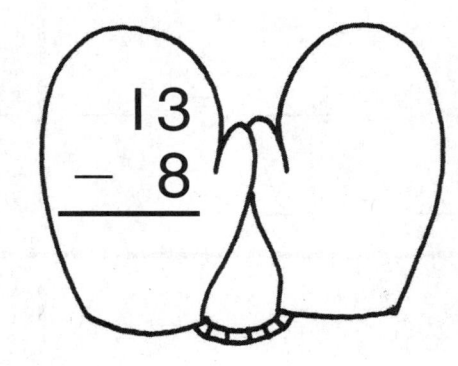

13 − 8

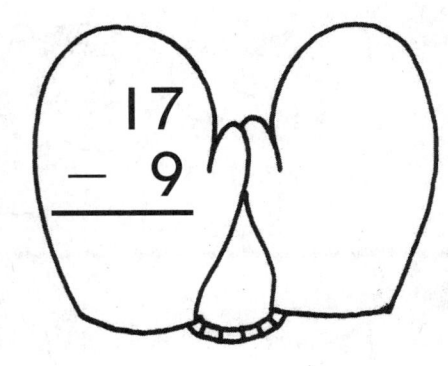

17 − 9

3.

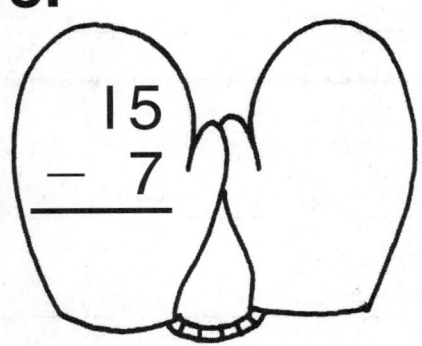

15 − 7

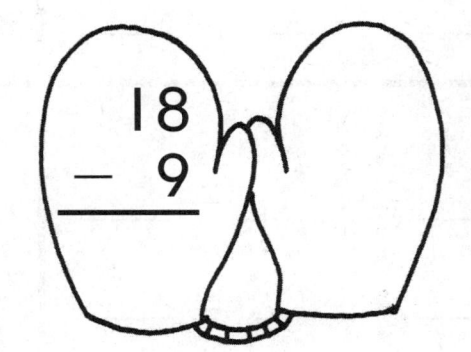

18 − 9

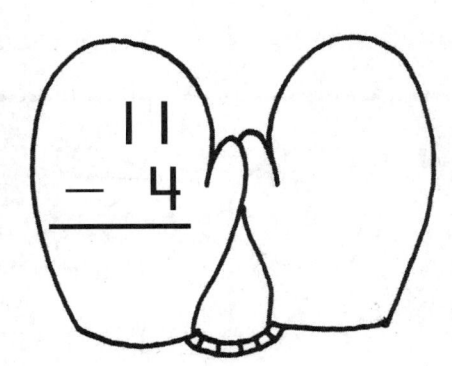

11 − 4

Name _____ Date _____

WRITING FACT FAMILIES
··
Family Ties

➡ Write each fact family.

1. (bow: 6, 7, 13) 6 + 7 = 13 | 7 + 6 = 13
   13 - 7 = 6 | 13 - 6 = 7

2. (bow: 6, 9, 15) ___ + ___ = ___ | ___ + ___ = ___
   ___ - ___ = ___ | ___ - ___ = ___

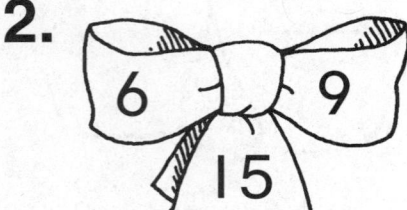

3. (bow: 8, 4, 12) ___ + ___ = ___ | ___ + ___ = ___
   ___ - ___ = ___ | ___ - ___ = ___

4. (bow: 6, 5, 11) ___ + ___ = ___ | ___ + ___ = ___
   ___ - ___ = ___ | ___ - ___ = ___

5. (bow: 9, 8, 17) ___ + ___ = ___ | ___ + ___ = ___
   ___ - ___ = ___ | ___ - ___ = ___

www.harcourtschoolsupply.com
© Harcourt Achieve Inc. All rights reserved.

Lesson 5, Addition and Subtraction to 18: Practice
Math: First Grade, SV 9937-6

Name _____ Date _____

ADDING AND SUBTRACTING NUMBERS

The Missing Bone

➡ Write the missing clues for Detective Diana.

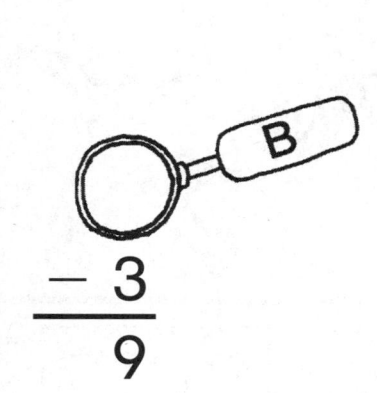

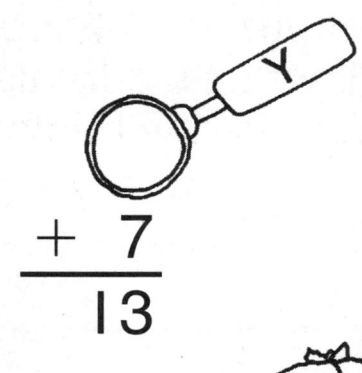

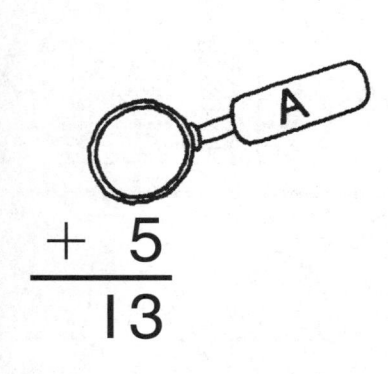

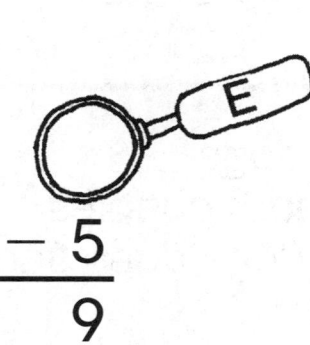

B
```
  ☐
- 3
———
  9
```

N
```
  ☐
+ 8
———
 15
```

Y
```
  ☐
+ 7
———
 13
```

A
```
  ☐
+ 5
———
 13
```

R
```
  ☐
- 9
———
  2
```

E
```
  ☐
- 5
———
  9
```

➡ Write the answer letter in each space.
Who lost his bone?

___ ___ ___ ___ ___ ___
12   8   11   7   14   6

Name _____ Date _____

SOLVING WORD PROBLEMS

Problems with Puppies

➡ Write each number sentence. Add or subtract.

1. There are 14 puppy treats in a box.
Spot eats 5 treats.
How many treats are left?

_____ ◯ _____ = _____ treats

2. There are 6 black puppies at the pet store.
There are 7 brown puppies, too.
How many puppies are there in all?

_____ ◯ _____ = _____ puppies

3. Jack has 3 dogs.
One dog had 8 puppies.
How many dogs does Jack have in all?

_____ ◯ _____ = _____ dogs

4. Ling's puppy is 17 weeks old.
She got it when it was 8 weeks old.
How many weeks has Ling had her puppy?

_____ ◯ _____ = _____ weeks

www.harcourtschoolsupply.com
© Harcourt Achieve Inc. All rights reserved.

Lesson 5, Addition and Subtraction to 18: Word Problems
Math: First Grade, SV 9937-6

Name _____ Date _____

Writing Number Sentences

➡ Write 6 number sentences that use the number shown in the flower.

(13) (15)

Name _____ Date _____

Adding Patterns

➡ Choose 3 colors of connecting cubes. Get 18 cubes in all. Make a pattern. Write a number sentence to show the cubes. Draw the pattern.

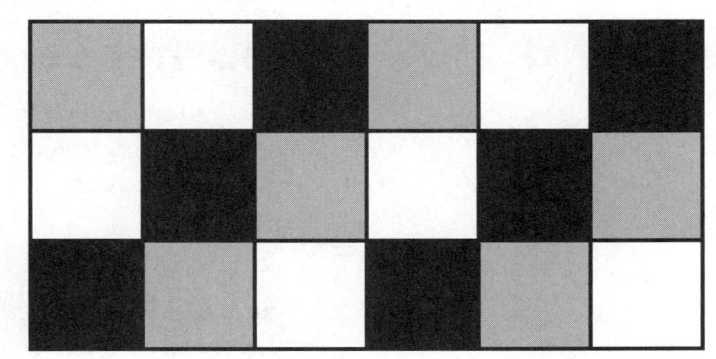

Example

_____ + _____ + _____ = 18

Lesson 6

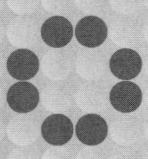

Patterns

Objectives

- Sort, classify, and order objects by size, number, and other properties
- Recognize, describe, and extend patterns such as sequences of sounds and shapes or simple numeric patterns and translate from one representation to another
- Analyze how both repeating and growing patterns are generated
- Apply and adapt a variety of appropriate strategies to solve problems

Materials

- connecting cubes, crayons, pencils, pattern blocks (optional), circle-shaped colored cereal (optional), yarn cut into 18-inch lengths (optional), 100 Chart blackline on page 126 (optional), wallpaper or fabric (optional), self-sealing plastic bags (optional), several kinds of dried beans (optional)

Lesson Pages

Page 48 (Manipulatives)
Children use 2 colors of connecting cubes to make a pattern on a path. Encourage more than just an AB pattern. Extend the activity to include more colors, shape patterns (using pattern blocks), and number patterns.

Page 49 (Practice)
Children follow directions to color and complete a color pattern.

Page 50 (Practice)
Children draw the size of the shape that comes next in the pattern.

Page 51 (Extension)
To help understand that there are patterns all around, children circle patterns they see in a picture.

Page 52 (Word Problems)
Children solve word problems about patterns.

Page 53 (Enrichment)
Activity Card 1: Children use crayons to color a design.
Activity Card 2: Children use pattern blocks to make a picture and have a friend make the pattern.

Another Look

- Use pattern blocks to build shape patterns. Have partners work together to describe and extend the pattern. (Visual, Kinesthetic, Auditory, ELL)
- Provide circle-shaped colored cereal and yarn cut into 18-inch lengths. Invite children to use the cereal to make a color-patterned necklace. (Visual, Kinesthetic, ELL)

Extension

- Using the 100 Chart on page 126, write numbers to 100. Give directions to help children notice number patterns. For example, say: *Color all numbers ending in 2 blue. Color all numbers that have a 6 in the tens place green.* Challenge children to notice other patterns.

- Display several sheets of wallpaper from recycled books or patterned fabric squares. Invite children to describe the color and shape patterns they see.

At Home

- Send home self-sealing bags with two kinds of dried beans. Have children use the beans to make patterns and describe them. Suggest that they have a family member make patterns that the children can extend and describe.

- Ask children to go on a pattern hunt for numbers. Ask them to take a walk with a family member and look for number patterns on mailboxes, houses, and streets.

- Visit www.harcourtachieve.com/achievementzone for additional ideas and activity pages.

Answer Key

Page 48
Answer will vary.

Page 49
1. red, yellow
2. green, red
3. purple, red
4. blue, blue

Page 50
1. large square
2. large square
3. large square
4. very small square

Children order the square cutouts from small to large.

Page 51
Children find the 5 patterns:
1. the zebra's mane (black and white)
2. the clothes on the line (shirt, 2 shoes)
3. the pattern on the shirts (triangle, circle)
4. the stripes on the chair (thin, thick)
5. the apples on the tree (in 3s)

Page 52
1. Children circle the hearts in the first row with the pattern white heart, black heart.
2. The pattern is count by 5.
3. 6
4. Children circle the spotted bead.

Page 53
Card 1: Answers will vary.
Card 2: Answers will vary.

Name _____ Date _____

IDENTIFYING PATTERNS

Stepping Stone Play

➡ **Make a pattern for the path. Use 2 colors of cubes. Lay the cubes on the stones. Ask a friend to tell the pattern.**

www.harcourtschoolsupply.com
© Harcourt Achieve Inc. All rights reserved.

48

Lesson 6, Patterns: Manipulatives
Math: First Grade, SV 9937-6

Name _____ Date _____

EXTENDING COLOR PATTERNS

Coloring Colors

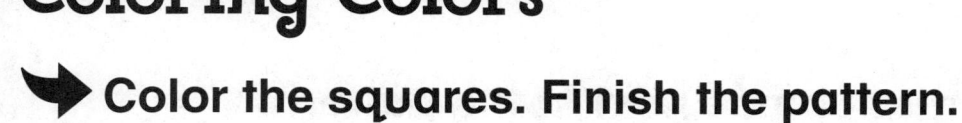

➡ **Color the squares. Finish the pattern.**

1.

red	yellow	red	yellow	red	yellow	red	yellow
						red	yellow

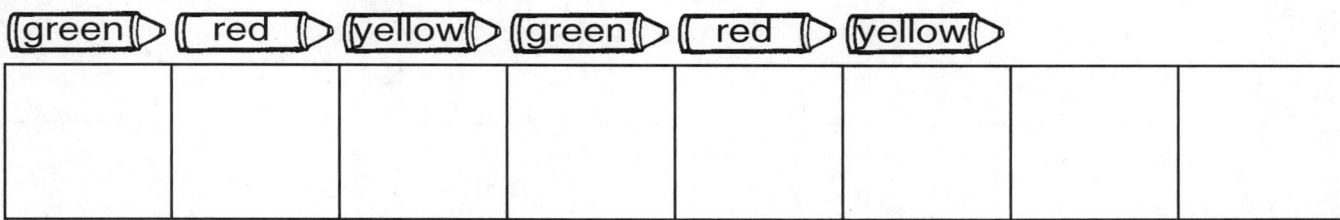

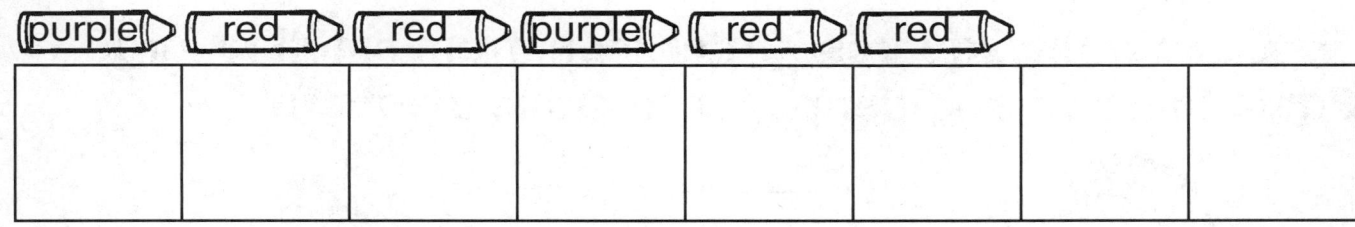

2.

green	red	yellow	green	red	yellow		

3.

purple	red	red	purple	red	red		

4.

red	red	blue	blue	red	red		

www.harcourtschoolsupply.com
© Harcourt Achieve Inc. All rights reserved.

49

Lesson 6, Patterns: Practice
Math: First Grade, SV 9937-6

Name _____ Date _____

EXTENDING SIZE PATTERNS

Next Size

➤ Draw the one that comes next in the pattern.

1.

2.

3.

4.

➤ Cut out the squares. Order them from small to large. Paste them on another paper to make a pattern.

www.harcourtschoolsupply.com
© Harcourt Achieve Inc. All rights reserved.

Lesson 6, Patterns: Practice
Math: First Grade, SV 9937-6

Name _____   Date _____

FINDING PATTERNS

Hide and Seek Patterns

➡ Find 5 patterns. Circle them.

51

www.harcourtschoolsupply.com
© Harcourt Achieve Inc. All rights reserved.

Lesson 6, Patterns: Extension
Math: First Grade, SV 9937-6

Name _____ Date _____

SOLVING WORD PROBLEMS

Patterns All Around

➡ **Read each story. Solve.**

1. Lena drew hearts.
Circle the row that shows a pattern.

♡ ♥ ♡ ♥ ♡ ♥

♡ ♡ ♡ ♥ ♡ ♥

2. Ben counted some numbers.
Write the number pattern.

5, 10, 15, 20, 25, 30, 35, 40, 45, 50

The pattern is _____

3. A number fell off the second door.
What number is it? Write the number on the door.

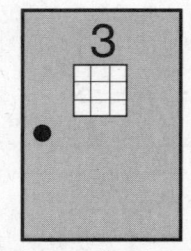

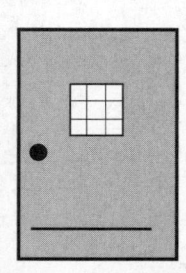

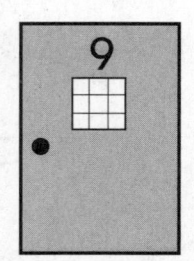

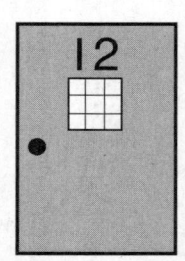

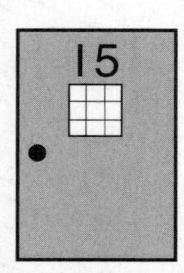

3   ___   9   12   15

4. Lisa is making a necklace.
What bead will come next? Circle it.

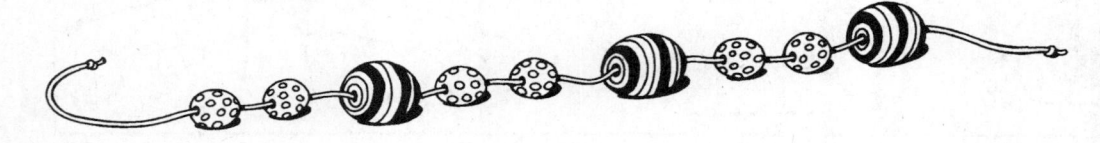

---

www.harcourtschoolsupply.com
© Harcourt Achieve Inc. All rights reserved.

52

Lesson 6, Patterns: Word Problems
Math: First Grade, SV 9937-6

Name _____ Date _____

Coloring a Pattern

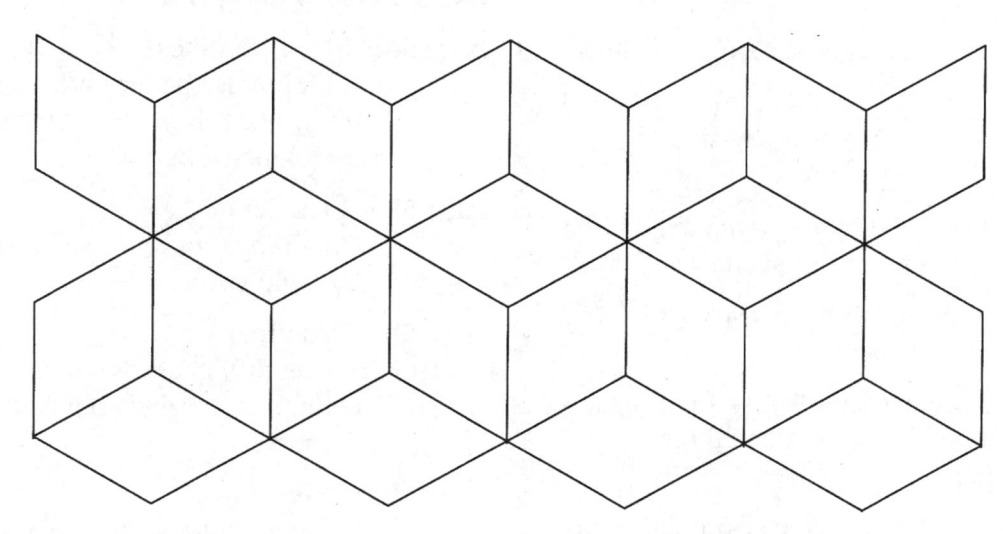

➤ **Color in some shapes to make a pattern.**

Name _____ Date _____

Making Pattern Pictures

➤ **Work with a friend. Get pattern blocks. Make a design. Have your friend copy it.**

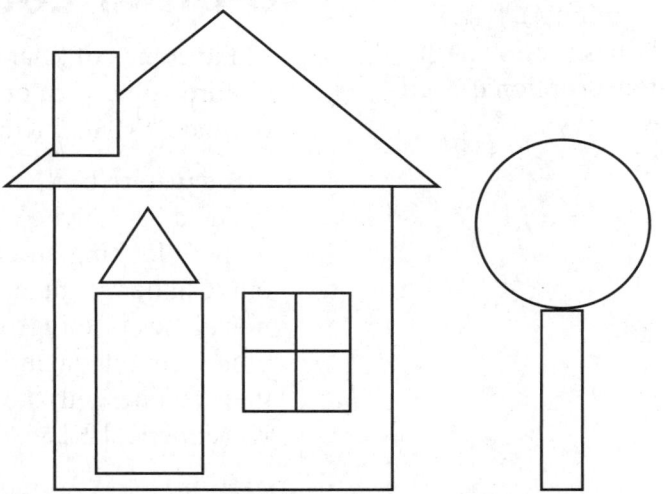

www.harcourtschoolsupply.com
© Harcourt Achieve Inc. All rights reserved.

Lesson 6, Patterns: Enrichment
Math: First Grade, SV 9937-6

Lesson 7

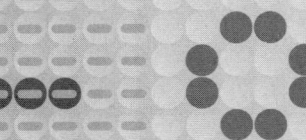

Plane Figures

Objectives

- Count with understanding and recognize "how many" in sets of objects
- Sort, classify, and order objects by size, number, and other properties
- Recognize, name, build, draw, compare, and sort two- and three-dimensional shapes
- Describe attributes and parts of two- and three-dimensional shapes
- Investigate and predict the results of putting together and taking apart two- and three-dimensional shapes
- Recognize and represent shapes from different perspectives
- Recognize geometric shapes and structures in the environment and specify their location
- Apply and adapt a variety of appropriate strategies to solve problems

Materials

- colored pattern blocks, pencils, crayons, scissors, glue, construction paper, toothpicks, Shapes blackline on page 127 (optional), yarn (optional), 100 Chart blackline on page 126 (optional), number cubes (optional), bags (optional), recycled magazines (optional), a variety of small shape cutouts (optional), self-sealing plastic bags (optional)

Lesson Pages

Page 56 (Manipulatives)
Children use pattern blocks to make a train. Then they count the number of each kind of figure.

Page 57 (Practice)
Children color figures that are the same size and shape.

Page 58 (Practice)
To identify characteristics of figures, children color and count sides and corners.

Page 59 (Extension)
Children color and cut out shapes. Then they glue the shapes to make a robot.

Page 60 (Word Problems)
Children follow instructions and solve word problems.

Page 61 (Enrichment)
Activity Card 1: Children build many different figures using 8 toothpicks and draw the shapes to record them.
Activity Card 2: Children color figures having 6 sides in a design.

Another Look

- Make copies of Shapes on page 127. Have children glue yarn on the sides to trace the outlines. (Visual, Kinesthetic, ELL)

- Place pattern blocks, one for each child, inside a bag. Invite children to choose a shape without looking and name it before pulling it out. Challenge them to cut out pictures from magazines of things having that shape and glue them on paper. Remind them to label their picture with the shape name. (Visual, Kinesthetic, ELL)

Extension

- Make copies of the 100 Chart on page 126. Then give partners a number cube. Have children take turns rolling the cube and drawing a figure with that number of sides on the chart. Challenge them to draw as many figures on the chart as they can without overlapping.

- Invite children to select and identify one of each colored pattern block. Have them lay the blocks on their desks. Then say riddles about shapes that describe the sides and corners. Have children hold up the correct shape and say the name.

At Home

- Send home a variety of small shape cutouts in self-sealing bags. Have children glue the shapes to paper to create a picture. Ask them to share their picture with a family member and name the shapes they used.

- Challenge children to go on a food hunt to find 5 foods that have a shape they know. Ask them to draw the foods. If time permits during the following day, have them match colored shape blocks to the drawings.

- Visit www.harcourtachieve.com/achievementzone for additional ideas and activity pages.

Answer Key

Page 56
1. 5
2. 3
3. 8
4. 2

Page 57
1. Children color the first, third, and sixth figures.
2. Children color the first and seventh figures.
3. Children color the first, fourth, fifth, and sixth figures.
4. Children color the first, third, and seventh figures.

Page 58
Children color the corresponding sides and corners correctly.
1. 3, 3
2. 4, 4
3. 8, 8
4. 5, 5
5. 3, 3
6. 4, 4

Page 59
Robots will vary.

Page 60
1. Children color the circle.
2. Children color the triangle.
3. Children draw a rectangle.
4. 2

Page 61
Card 1: Answers will vary.

Card 2:

Name _____ Date _____

EXPLORING PLANE FIGURES

A Shapely Train

▶ Use pattern blocks. Make the train. Then write how many blocks.

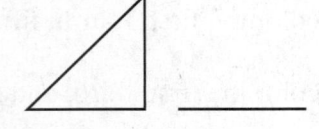

1. △ ____

2. ▭ ____

3. ○ ____

4. □ ____

Lesson 7, Plane Figures: Manipulatives
Math: First Grade, SV 9937-6

Name _____   Date _____

CLASSIFYING PLANE FIGURES
....

Size It Up

➡ Color the same size and shape.

1.

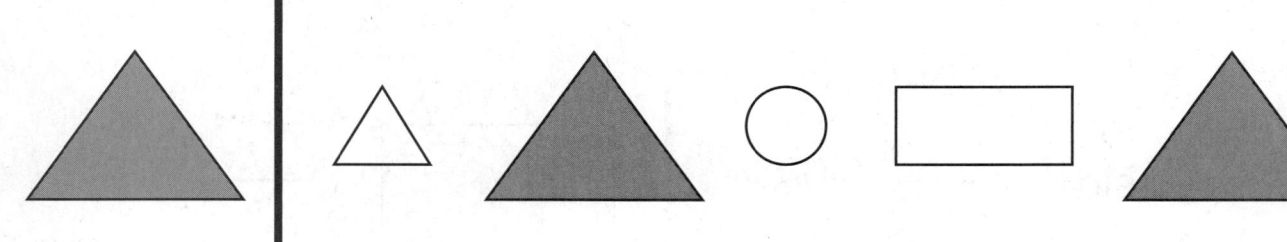

2.

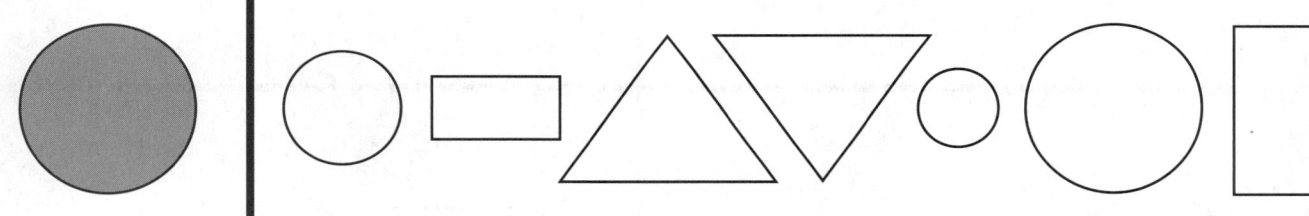

3.

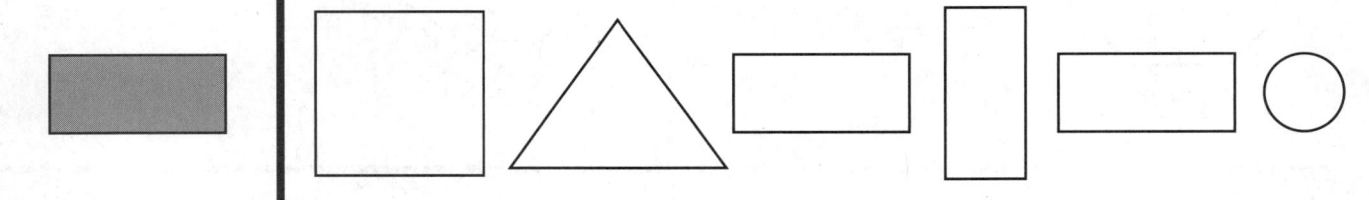

4.

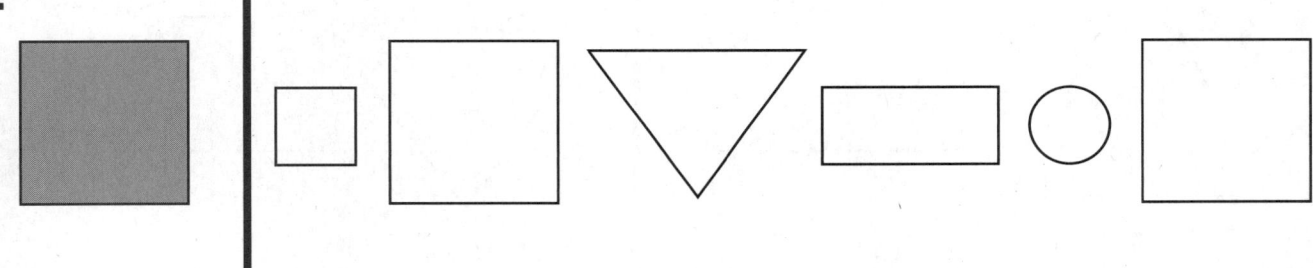

www.harcourtschoolsupply.com
© Harcourt Achieve Inc. All rights reserved.

Lesson 7, Plane Figures: Practice
Math: First Grade, SV 9937-6

Name _____ Date _____

IDENTIFYING SIDES AND CORNERS

These Corners Count

➤ Trace each side with the color blue. Draw a red circle on each corner. Write how many sides and corners.

1.

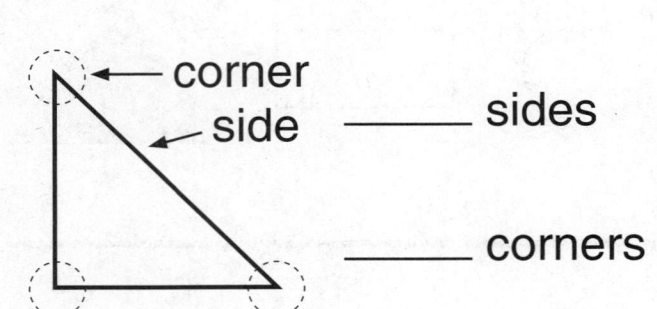

_____ sides

_____ corners

2.

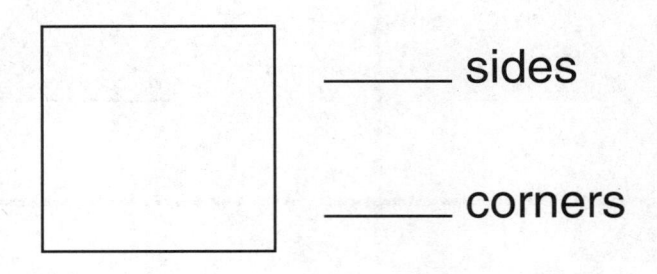

_____ sides

_____ corners

3.

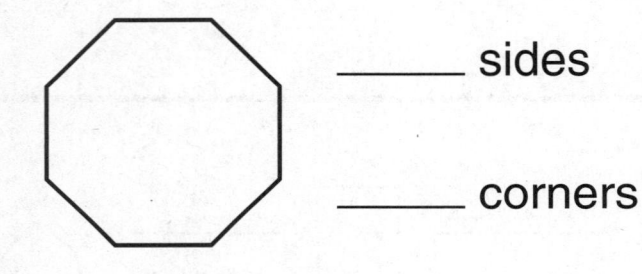

_____ sides

_____ corners

4.

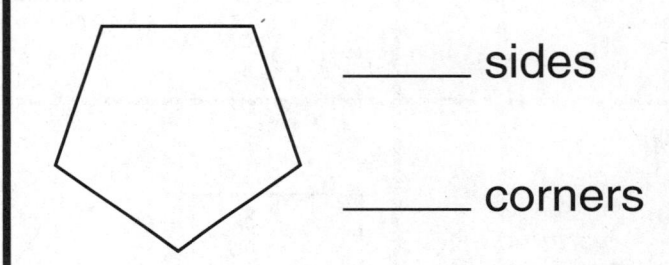

_____ sides

_____ corners

5.

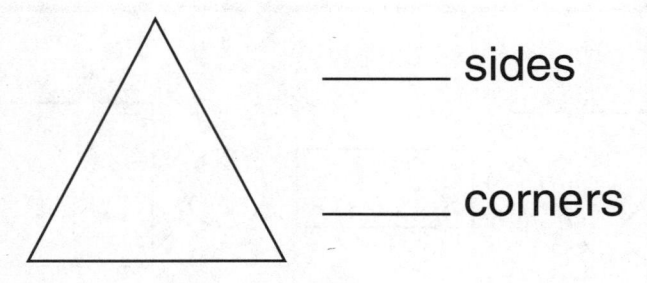

_____ sides

_____ corners

6.

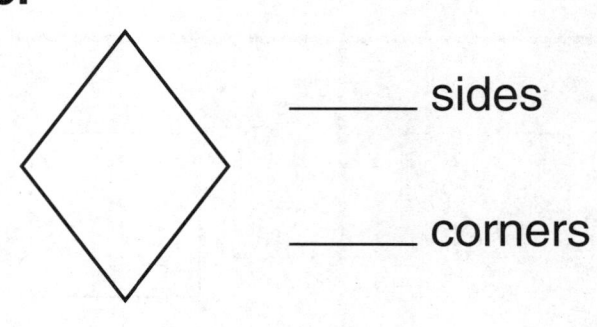

_____ sides

_____ corners

www.harcourtschoolsupply.com
© Harcourt Achieve Inc. All rights reserved.

58

Lesson 7, Plane Figures: Practice
Math: First Grade, SV 9937-6

Name _____ Date _____

BUILDING WITH PLANE FIGURES
••

A Shapely Robot

➤ **Color the shapes. Cut them out. Use all of the shapes to make a robot. Glue the robot on paper.**

www.harcourtschoolsupply.com

© Harcourt Achieve Inc. All rights reserved.

Lesson 7, Plane Figures: Extension
Math: First Grade, SV 9937-6

Name _____ Date _____

SOLVING WORD PROBLEMS

Shape Up

➤ **Read each story. Solve.**

1. Ann drew a circle. Which shape did Ann draw? Color it.

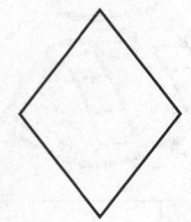

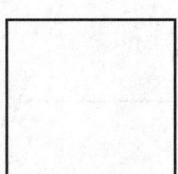

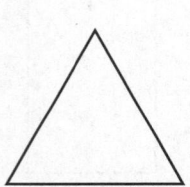

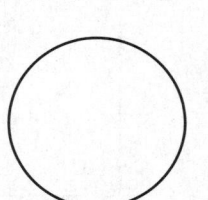

2. I have 3 sides. I have 3 corners. What am I? Color it.

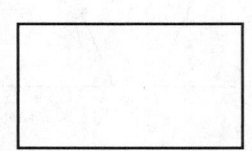

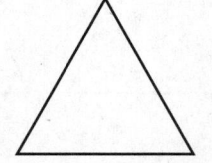

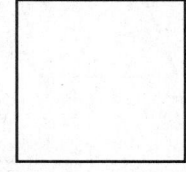

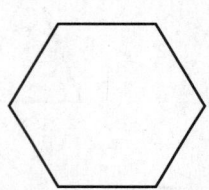

3. Lee planted a garden. It had 2 long sides and 2 short sides. What shape was Lee's garden? Draw it.

4. Tia made this picture with blocks. How many ☐ did she use?

Name _____ Date _____

Making Eight

➡ **Get 8 toothpicks.**
How many shapes can you make?
Draw them.

Name _____ Date _____

Looking for Six

➡ **Color each shape that has 6 sides.**

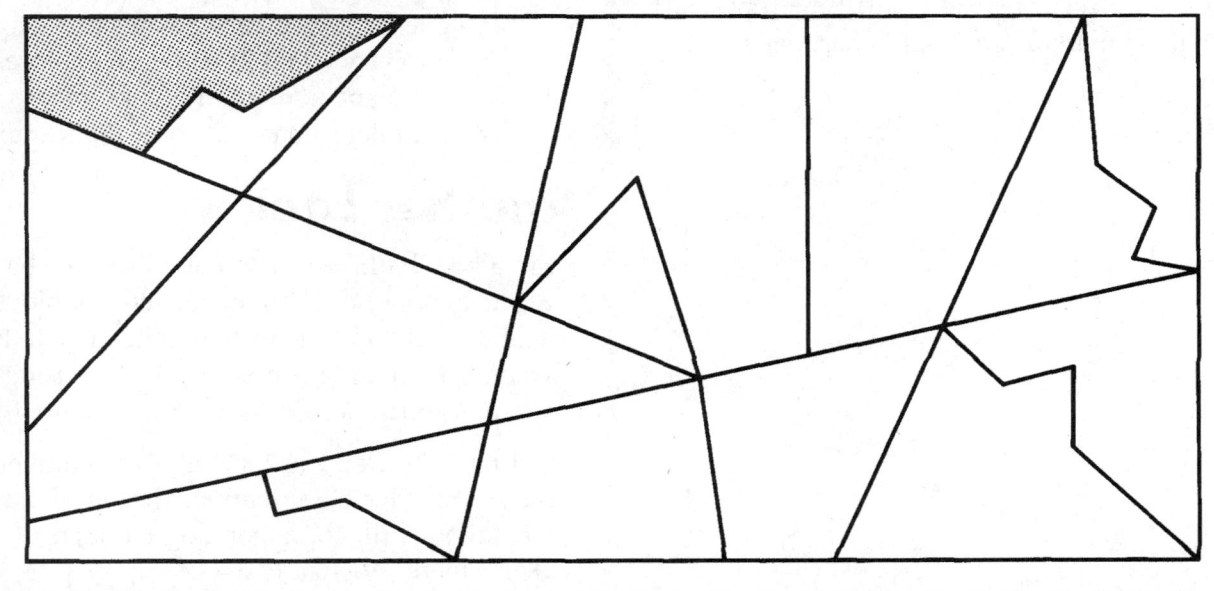

61

www.harcourtschoolsupply.com
© Harcourt Achieve Inc. All rights reserved.

Lesson 7, Plane Figures: Enrichment
Math: First Grade, SV 9937-6

Lesson 8

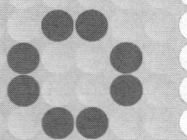

Solid Figures

Objectives

- Count with understanding and recognize "how many" in sets of objects
- Sort, classify, and order objects by size, number, and other properties
- Recognize, name, build, draw, compare, and sort two- and three-dimensional shapes
- Describe attributes and parts of two- and three-dimensional shapes
- Investigate and predict the results of putting together and taking apart two- and three-dimensional shapes
- Recognize and represent shapes from different perspectives
- Recognize geometric shapes and structures in the environment and specify their location
- Apply and adapt a variety of appropriate strategies to solve problems

Materials

- large three-dimensional shape blocks, pencils, crayons, grocery bag (optional), tape (optional), permanent marker (optional), chart paper (optional)

Lesson Pages

Page 64 (Manipulatives)
Children match shape blocks to items they often see around them.

Page 65 (Practice)
Discuss the labeled solid shapes in the middle column. Children draw lines from the labeled shapes to the matching shapes of familiar objects in the first and last columns.

Page 66 (Practice)
Children examine solids to develop an understanding of which shapes stack, roll, or slide.

Page 67 (Extension)
Children count the figures used to build a house and record the number to make a bar graph.

Page 68 (Word Problems)
Children solve word problems.

Page 69 (Enrichment)
Activity Card 1: Children look at cube buildings and use visual thinking to guess the number of cubes in each.
Activity Card 2: Children explore sides and corners of blocks and complete a chart to show their findings.

Another Look

- Put a box, ball, cone, and can block in a bag. Place another box, ball, cone, and can block on a table. Hold up a shape, name it, and challenge volunteers to find the block in the bag using their sense of touch only. (Visual, Kinesthetic, ELL)

- Get large blocks. Use tape labels to number the sides. Have children trace the sides and label them with corresponding numbers. (Kinesthetic, Visual, ELL)

Extension

- Put a box, ball, cone, and can block in a bag. Name a solid and have children find the block in the bag by using their sense of touch only.

- On chart paper, make a chart with these headings: *Roll, Slide, Stack*. Explain the words to children and model them using a cylinder block. Have children explore each solid and write a check under each heading if the figure has that attribute.

At Home

- Send home a paper that has a four-column chart on it. Include headings that show a box, ball, cone, and can. Challenge children to look around their house to find items that have these shapes. Ask them to draw pictures of the items in the appropriate column.

- Ask children to have a family member gather small containers and food boxes for them to sort.

- Visit www.harcourtachieve.com/ achievementzone for additional ideas and activity pages.

Answer Key

Page 64
1. cone   2. can   3. cone
4. box   5. ball   6. can
7. ball   8. box   9. box

Page 65
1. Children draw lines from the box to the block and ice cube.
2. Children draw lines from the ball to the baseball and globe.
3. Children draw lines from the cone to the megaphone and ice-cream cone.
4. Children draw lines from the can to the jar and glass.

Page 66
1. Children color the first, second, fourth, and fifth shapes.
2. Children color the second, third, and fourth shapes.
3. Children color the first, second, fourth, and fifth shapes.
4. Children color the first, second, and third shapes.

Page 67
Children color the picture and complete the graph as follows:
Cube: 8   Cone: 3
Cylinder: 5   Rectangular prism: 6

Page 68
1. Children color the cone.
2. Children color the pyramid.
3. 4 rectangles, 2 squares
4. Children color the sphere.

Page 69
Card 1:
1. 7   2. 12   3. 18

Card 2:

Shape	How many sides?	How many corners?
cube	6	8
sphere	0	0
cone	1	1
cylinder	2	0

Name _____ Date _____

EXPLORING SOLID FIGURES

Block Sort

➡ Get a ◯, ▢, ◁, and ▯. Match the blocks to the pictures.

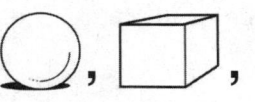

1.	2.	3.
4.	5.	6.
7.	8.	9.

www.harcourtschoolsupply.com
© Harcourt Achieve Inc. All rights reserved.

Lesson 8, Solid Figures: Manipulatives
Math: First Grade, SV 9937-6

Name _____ Date _____

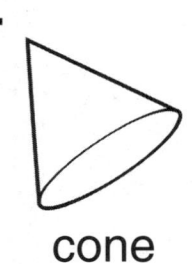

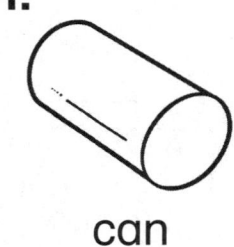

CLASSIFYING SOLID FIGURES
....

Solid Shapes

➡ Draw lines to match.

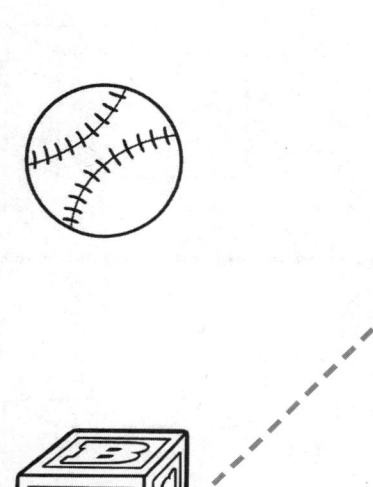

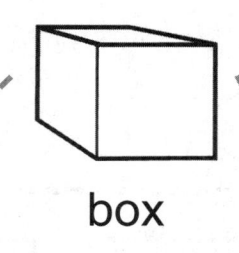

1. box

2. ball

3. cone

4. can

www.harcourtschoolsupply.com
© Harcourt Achieve Inc. All rights reserved.

65

Lesson 8, Solid Figures: Practice
Math: First Grade, SV 9937-6

Name _____   Date _____

UNDERSTANDING SOLID FIGURES

Stack, Roll, Slide

▶ 1. Color each shape that will stack.

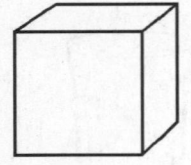

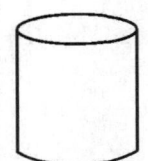

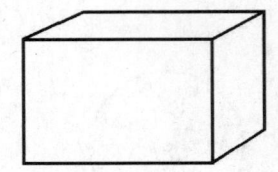

▶ 2. Color each shape that will roll.

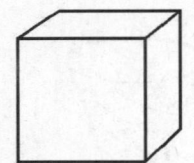

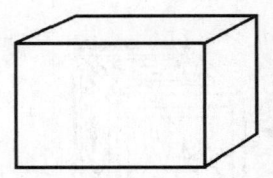

▶ 3. Color each shape that will slide.

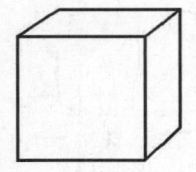

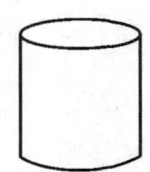

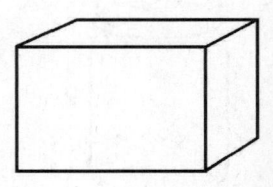

▶ 4. Use solid shapes to build. Color each shape that will stack.

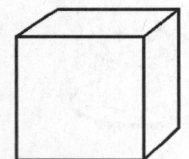

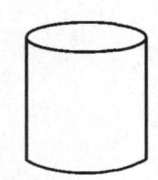

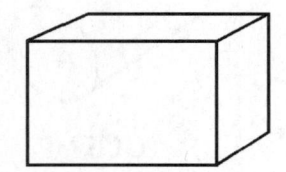

www.harcourtschoolsupply.com
© Harcourt Achieve Inc. All rights reserved.

Lesson 8, Solid Figures: Practice
Math: First Grade, SV 9937-6

Name _____ Date _____

COUNTING SOLID FIGURES

A Solid House

➡ **Count the shapes. Complete the graph.**

0 1 2 3 4 5 6 7 8

Lesson 8, Solid Figures: Extension
Math: First Grade, SV 9937-6

Name _____ Date _____

SOLVING WORD PROBLEMS

Blocks of Fun

➡ **Read each story. Solve.**

1. Ed uses these blocks to build.
   Which shape must he put on top?
   Color it.

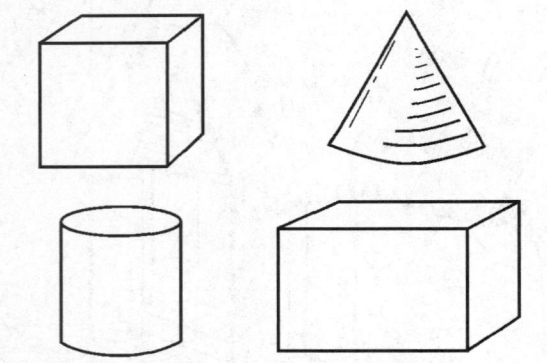

2. Kwan has a block.
   It has 1 square side.
   It has 4 triangle sides.
   Color the block.

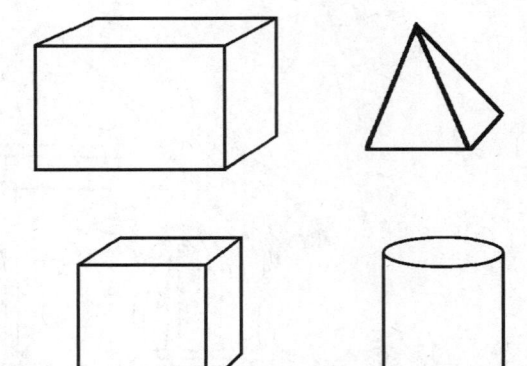

3. Rod has a box.
   He counts the sides.
   How many of each side does the box have?

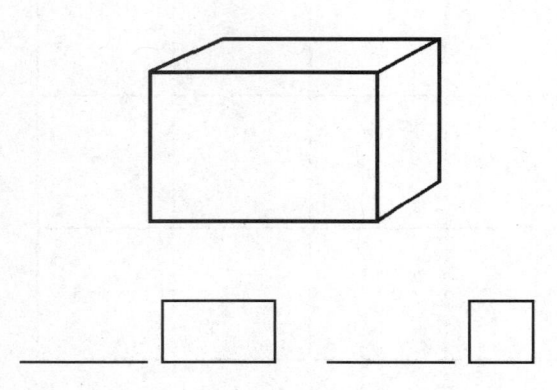

4. Eva gets a ball.
   What shape is the ball?
   Color it.

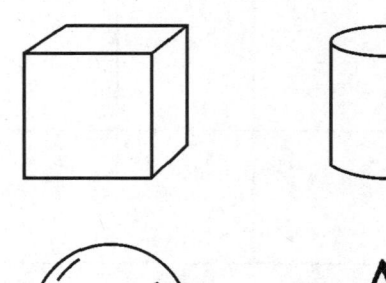

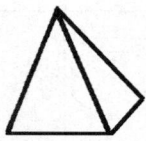

www.harcourtschoolsupply.com
© Harcourt Achieve Inc. All rights reserved.

68

Lesson 8, Solid Figures: Word Problems
Math: First Grade, SV 9937-6

Name _____ Date _____

Counting Cubes

➡ **Count the cubes. Write how many.**

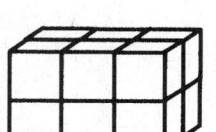

1.
2.
3.

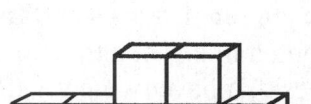

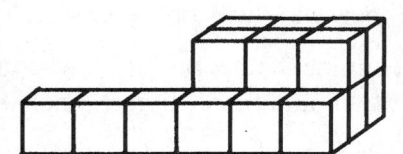

_____ cubes _____ cubes _____ cubes

Name _____ Date _____

Learning About Solids

➡ **Look at each shape. Count the sides.
Count the corners. Write the numbers in the chart.**

Parts of Solids

Shape	How many sides?	How many corners?
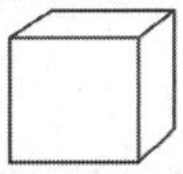		

www.harcourtschoolsupply.com
© Harcourt Achieve Inc. All rights reserved.

Lesson 8, Solid Figures: Enrichment
Math: First Grade, SV 9937-6

Lesson 9

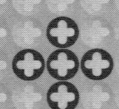

Symmetry

Objectives

- Sort, classify, and order objects by size, number, and other properties
- Recognize, name, build, draw, compare, and sort two- and three-dimensional shapes
- Describe attributes and parts of two- and three-dimensional shapes
- Investigate and predict the results of putting together and taking apart two- and three-dimensional shapes
- Recognize and create shapes that have symmetry
- Recognize and represent shapes from different perspectives
- Apply and adapt a variety of appropriate strategies to solve problems

Materials

- scissors, pencils, crayons, construction paper (optional), recycled magazines (optional), self-sealing plastic bags (optional), dried beans (optional)

Lesson Pages

Page 72 (Manipulatives)
Children cut out 4 shapes and fold them along a line. Then they identify the shapes that have two parts that match.

Page 73 (Practice)
Children decide whether shapes have equal parts.

Page 74 (Practice)
Children draw lines of symmetry.

Page 75 (Extension)
Children draw the missing half of the rabbit.

Page 76 (Word Problems)
Children solve word problems about symmetry.

Page 77 (Enrichment)
Activity Card 1: Children find letters of the alphabet that show symmetry.
Activity Card 2: Children look for all the lines of symmetry in a square.

Another Look

- Cut out large, simple shapes from construction paper. Cut them in half. Have children match the shapes to see the lines of symmetry. (Visual, Kinesthetic, ELL)

- Cut out shapes from construction paper. Fold some equally and some unequally. Have children sort the shapes. (Visual, Kinesthetic, ELL)

Extension

- Have children cut out 3 food items from recycled magazines. Have them draw a line of symmetry on the pictures.
- Invite children to fold a square of paper into fourths and cut out small shapes to make snowflakes.

At Home

- Send home dried beans in self-sealing bags. Have children glue the beans on paper to make a symmetrical design.
- Tell children to find ways to cut food so the parts show symmetry. They can cut sandwiches, apples, and fruit bars.
- Visit www.harcourtachieve.com/achievementzone for additional ideas and activity pages.

Answer Key

Page 72
Children identify the triangle and circle as having parts that match.

Page 73
1. no   2. yes   3. yes
4. no   5. yes   6. yes

Page 74
Children draw a line of symmetry on each picture.

Page 75
Children draw the other half of the rabbit.

Page 76
1. Children draw the other half of the tree.
2. Children circle the diamond.
3. Children circle the third card.
4. Children draw a line of symmetry.

Page 77
Card 1: Answers will vary but could include A, B, C, D, E, H, I, K, M, O, T, V, W, X, Y.
Card 2:

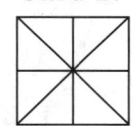

Name _____ Date _____

UNDERSTANDING SYMMETRY

Folding Fun

➡ **Cut out the shapes. Fold them on the line. Which shapes have two parts that match?**

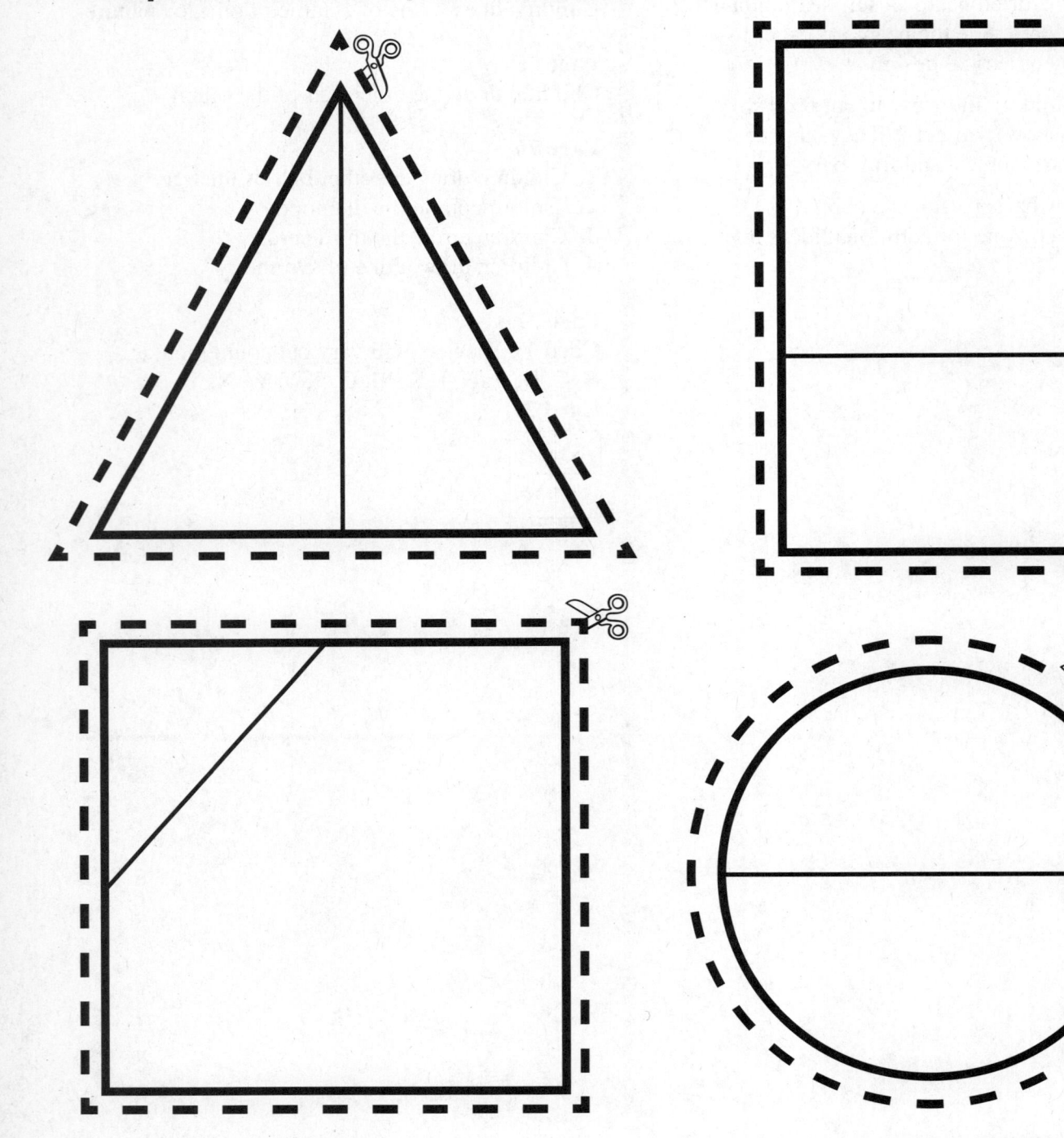

www.harcourtschoolsupply.com
© Harcourt Achieve Inc. All rights reserved.

Lesson 9, Symmetry: Manipulatives
Math: First Grade, SV 9937-6

Name _____   Date _____

IDENTIFYING SYMMETRY

The Great Shape Divide

➡ Do the two parts match? Circle <u>yes</u> or <u>no</u>.

1.

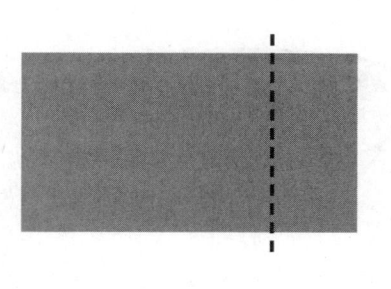

yes   (no)

2.

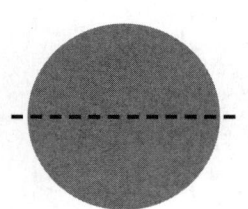

yes   no

3.

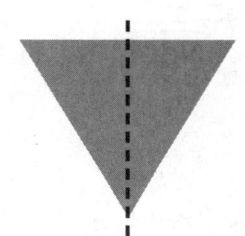

yes   no

4.

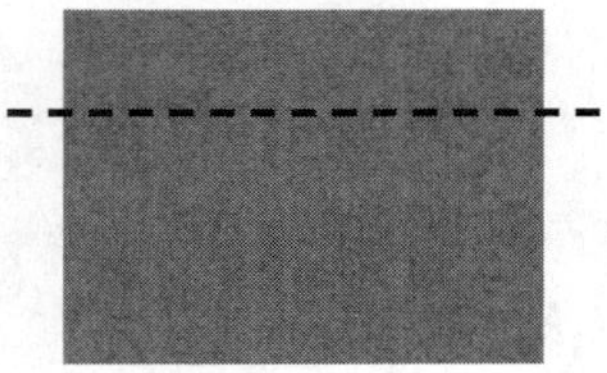

yes   no

5.

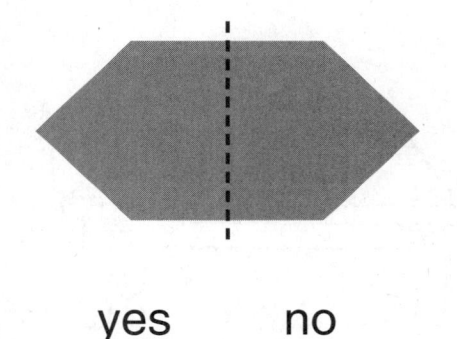

yes   no

6.

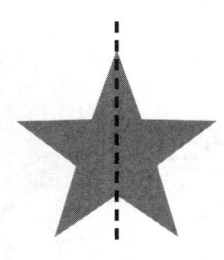

yes   no

www.harcourtschoolsupply.com
© Harcourt Achieve Inc. All rights reserved.

73

Lesson 9, Symmetry: Practice
Math: First Grade, SV 9937-6

Name _____ Date _____

PRACTICING SYMMETRY
Drawing the Line

➡ **Draw a line to make two parts that match.**

1.

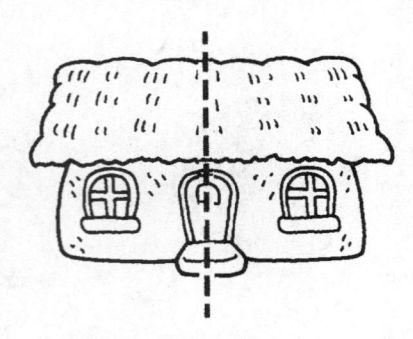

2.

3.

4.

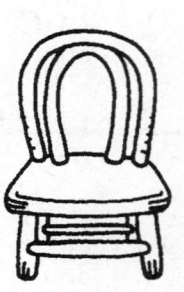

5.

6.

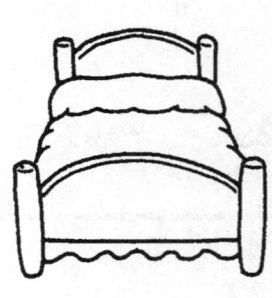

7.

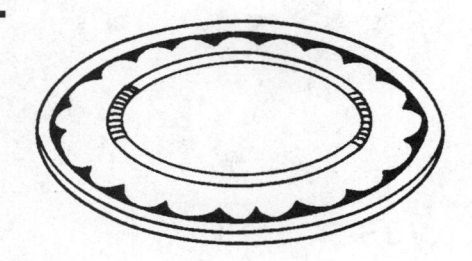

8.

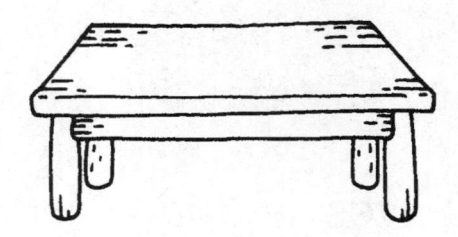

www.harcourtschoolsupply.com
© Harcourt Achieve Inc. All rights reserved.

Lesson 9, Symmetry: Practice
Math: First Grade, SV 9937-6

Name _____ Date _____

DRAWING SYMMETRICALLY

Ready Rabbit

➡ **Draw the rabbit. Make the parts the same.**

Name _____ Date _____

SOLVING WORD PROBLEMS

All the Same

➤ **Read each story. Solve.**

1. Sal draws a tree.
   What will it look like?
   Draw the tree to make
   it match.

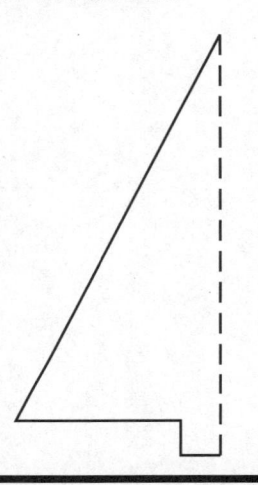

2. Amy cuts this paper.
   What does the shape that
   is cut look like when it is
   opened?
   Circle it.

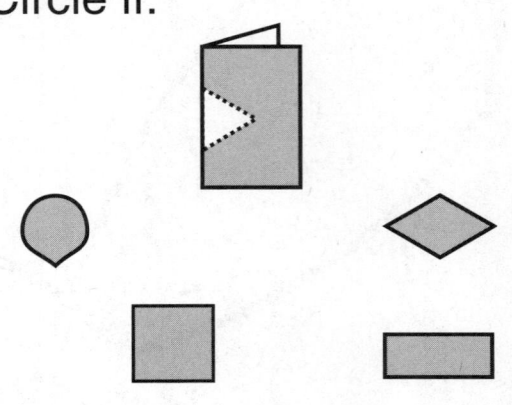

3. Inga makes this card.
   Which card makes a match?
   Circle it.

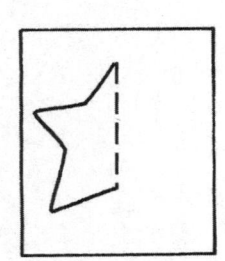

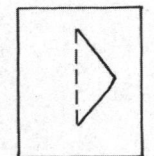

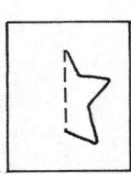

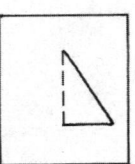

4. Sam cuts out a heart.
   He wants to make a card.
   Where will he fold it to
   make it match?
   Draw a line.

www.harcourtschoolsupply.com
© Harcourt Achieve Inc. All rights reserved.

76

Lesson 9, Symmetry: Word Problems
Math: First Grade, SV 9937-6

Name _____ Date _____

Finding Letter Symmetry

➤ Think about the letters in the alphabet. Which letters are symmetrical? Write the letters below.

Name _____ Date _____

Making Symmetry

➤ How many lines can you draw to make matching parts?

Lesson 9, Symmetry: Enrichment
Math: First Grade, SV 9937-6

Lesson 10

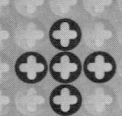

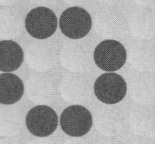

Fractions

Objectives

- Understand and represent commonly used fractions, such as $\frac{1}{4}$, $\frac{1}{3}$, and $\frac{1}{2}$
- Recognize, describe, and extend patterns such as sequences of sounds and shapes or simple numeric patterns and translate from one representation to another
- Analyze how both repeating and growing patterns are generated
- Investigate and predict the results of putting together and taking apart two- and three-dimensional shapes
- Recognize and represent shapes from different perspectives
- Apply and adapt a variety of appropriate strategies to solve problems

Materials

- scissors, pencils/crayons, glue, playground ball (optional), chalk (optional), colorful picture (optional), index cards (optional), markers (optional), connecting cubes (optional), plastic cups (optional)

Lesson Pages

Page 80 (Manipulatives)
Children cut out figures and fold them on the dotted lines to show halves, thirds, and fourths. You may have children form groups of two, three, and four and write their group members' names on the different parts to show equal shares.

Page 81 (Practice)
Children circle fractions to show the shaded parts of figures.

Page 82 (Practice)
Children color figures to show the given fraction.

Page 83 (Extension)
Children cut out pizzas and glue them in boxes, matching the divided pizzas to the number of people in each group.

Page 84 (Word Problems)
Children solve word problems about fractions.

Page 85 (Enrichment)
Activity Card 1: Children look at a fraction pattern and draw the next part as well as name the rule.
Activity Card 2: Children draw lines to match fractional parts of time to the movement of a clock.

www.harcourtschoolsupply.com
© Harcourt Achieve Inc. All rights reserved.

Lesson 10, Fractions: Teacher Information
Math: First Grade, SV 9937-6

Another Look

- Invite children to play a version of Four Square. Use chalk to draw 3 large circles on the playground and divide them into halves, thirds, and fourths. Allow each child to play on each court. Have them identify how the circle is divided before they can play. (Visual, Kinesthetic, ELL)

- Choose a colorful picture and duplicate it in color 3 times. Cut each picture to show halves, thirds, or fourths. Invite children to put the puzzles together and decide the fractional parts showing. (Visual, Kinesthetic, ELL)

Extension

- Make numeral cards and shape cards to show the fractions on page 82. Invite children to play Concentration to match the shape card to the numeral card.

- Using the numeral cards from above, put different colored connecting cubes, which are not connected, into plastic cups to match the fractions. Invite children to match the cards and cups.

At Home

- Ask children to choose a picture from a magazine or newspaper. Tell them to cut it into 2, 3, or 4 equal pieces to make a puzzle. Have children tell a family member if the puzzle is in halves, thirds, or fourths.

- Tell children to look for ways to divide food items into halves, thirds, and fourths. For snack, they can cut apples, oranges, and even peanut butter sandwiches.

- Visit www.harcourtachieve.com/achievementzone for additional ideas and activity pages.

Answer Key

Page 80
Children cut out and fold figures to show halves, thirds, and fourths.

Page 81
1. $\frac{1}{3}$ 2. $\frac{1}{3}$ 3. $\frac{1}{2}$
4. $\frac{1}{2}$ 5. $\frac{1}{4}$ 6. $\frac{1}{3}$
7. $\frac{1}{4}$ 8. $\frac{1}{2}$ 9. $\frac{1}{4}$

Page 82
Children color the following:
1. 1 part   2. 1 part   3. 2 parts
4. 1 part   5. 2 parts 6. 3 parts
7. 1 part   8. 2 parts 9. 3 parts

Page 83
Children glue the following pizzas:
1. thirds
2. halves
3. fourths

Page 84
1. Children circle the apple cut in halves.
2. $\frac{1}{3}$
3. $\frac{1}{4}$
4. Children color 1 pie.

Page 85
Card 1: Children draw lines to show sixths and color $\frac{1}{6}$. The rule is to divide the next circle into one more piece and color one part.
Card 2: Children draw lines from the clock to these times:
1. $\frac{1}{2}$ past the hour
2. $\frac{1}{4}$ past the hour
3. $\frac{3}{4}$ past the hour

Name _____ Date _____

UNDERSTANDING FRACTIONS

Fraction Folds

➥ **Cut out each shape. Fold each shape on the line. How many parts?**

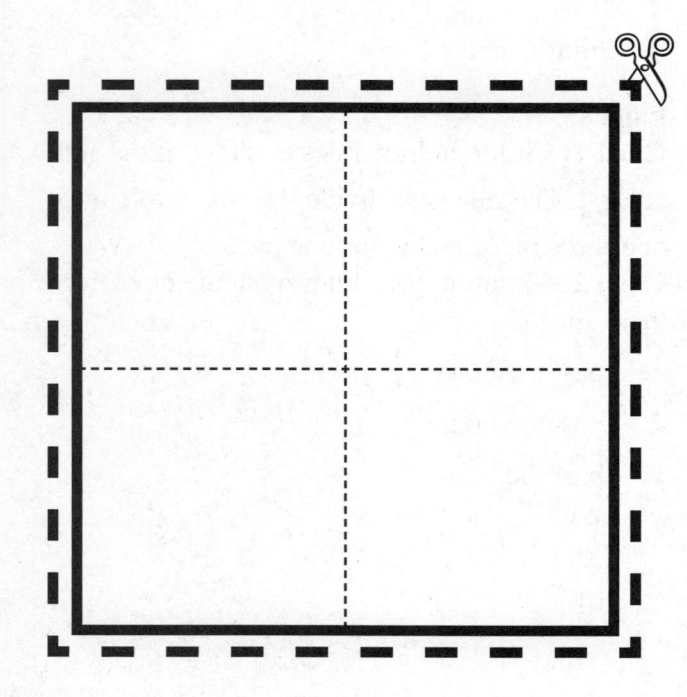

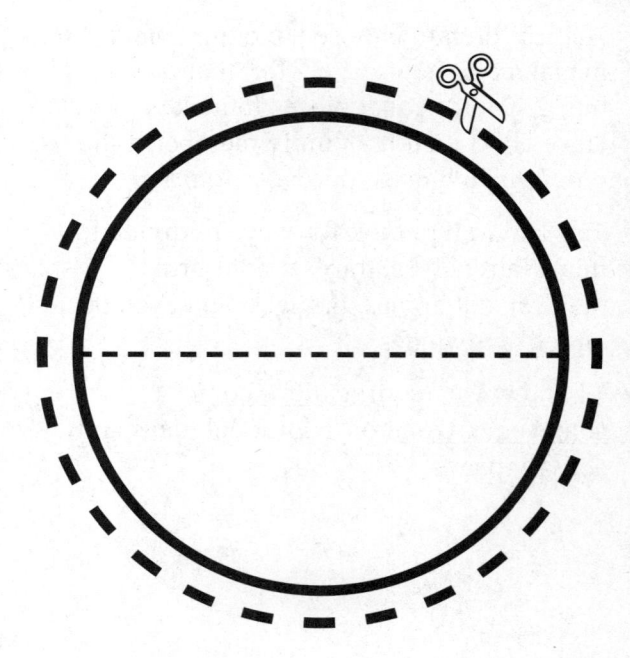

Lesson 10, Fractions: Manipulatives
Math: First Grade, SV 9937-6

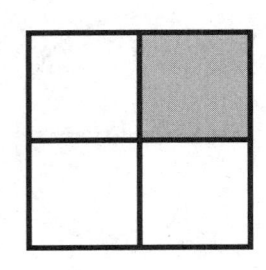

Name _____   Date _____

READING FRACTIONS

Fraction Action

➤ Circle the fraction each shape shows.

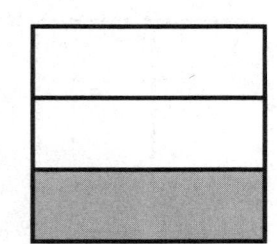

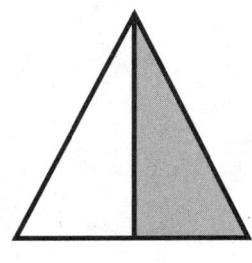

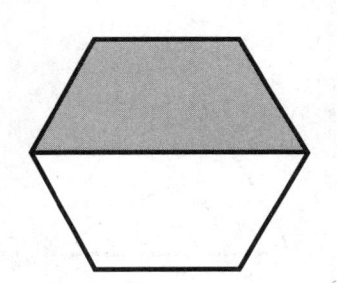

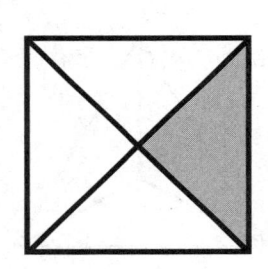

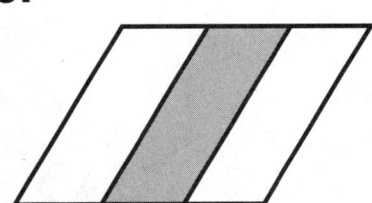

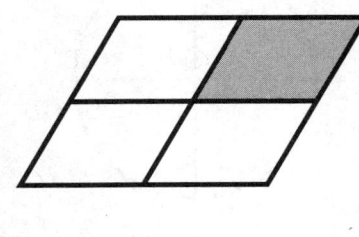

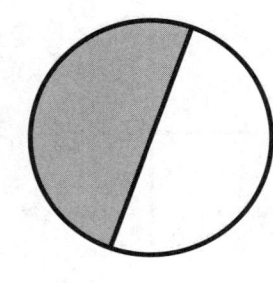

1.	2.	3.
$\frac{1}{2}$ ($\frac{1}{3}$)	$\frac{1}{2}$ $\frac{1}{3}$	$\frac{1}{2}$ $\frac{1}{3}$
4.	5.	6.
$\frac{1}{2}$ $\frac{1}{3}$	$\frac{1}{4}$ $\frac{1}{3}$	$\frac{1}{2}$ $\frac{1}{3}$
7.	8.	9.
$\frac{1}{4}$ $\frac{1}{3}$	$\frac{1}{2}$ $\frac{1}{3}$	$\frac{1}{4}$ $\frac{1}{3}$

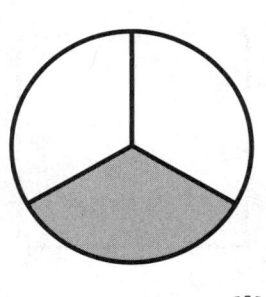

www.harcourtschoolsupply.com

© Harcourt Achieve Inc. All rights reserved.

Lesson 10, Fractions: Practice
Math: First Grade, SV 9937-6

Name _____ Date _____

COLORING FRACTIONS

Show Your Colors

➢ **Color to show the fraction.**

1.

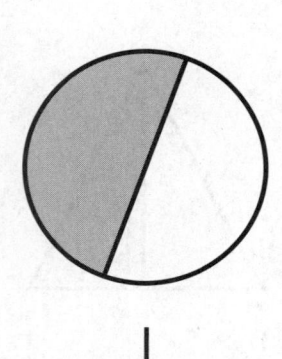

$\dfrac{1}{2}$

2.

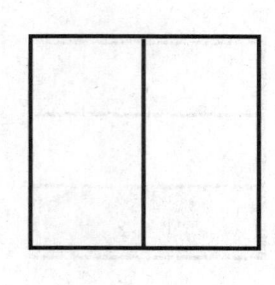

$\dfrac{1}{2}$

3.

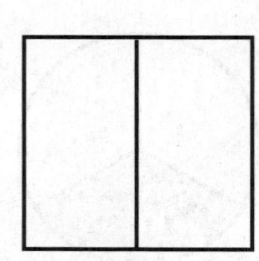

$\dfrac{2}{2}$

4.

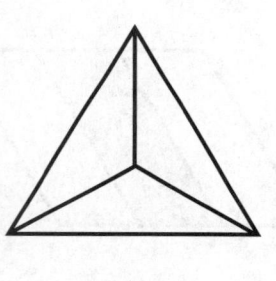

$\dfrac{1}{3}$

5.

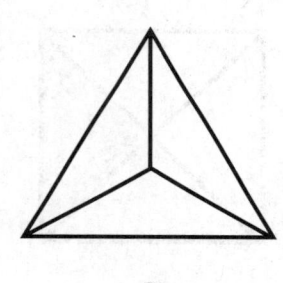

$\dfrac{2}{3}$

6.

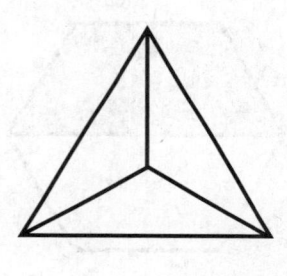

$\dfrac{3}{3}$

7.

$\dfrac{1}{4}$

8.

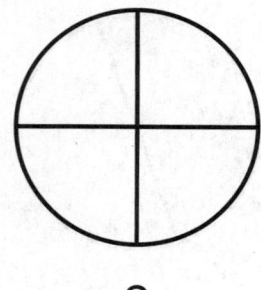

$\dfrac{2}{4}$

9.

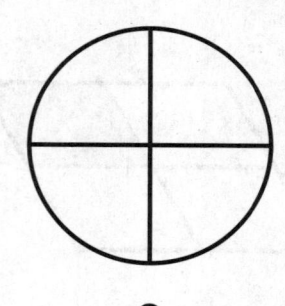

$\dfrac{3}{4}$

www.harcourtschoolsupply.com
© Harcourt Achieve Inc. All rights reserved.

Lesson 10, Fractions: Practice
Math: First Grade, SV 9937-6

Name _____ Date _____

FINDING FRACTIONAL PARTS

Pizza Parties

➡ Cut out the pizzas. Who gets each pizza? Glue it in the box.

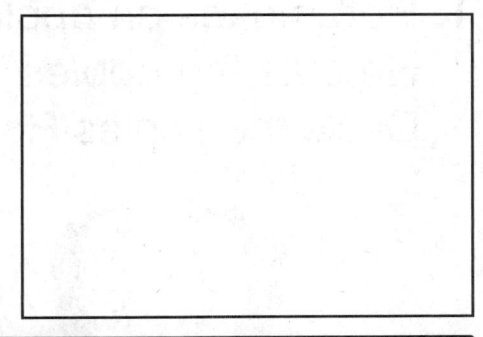

1.

2.

3.

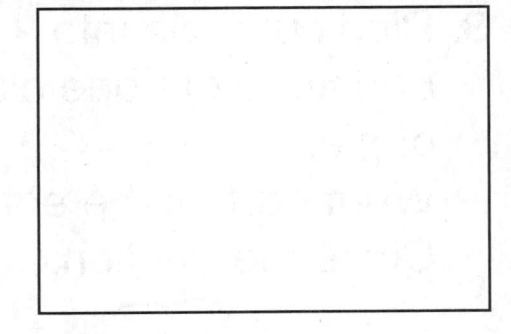

www.harcourtschoolsupply.com
© Harcourt Achieve Inc. All rights reserved.

Lesson 10, Fractions: Extension
Math: First Grade, SV 9937-6

Name _____ Date _____

SOLVING WORD PROBLEMS
···

It's as Easy as Pie

➡ **Read each story. Solve.**

1. Rob makes an apple pie.
   He cuts the apples in half.
   Circle the apples Rob cuts.

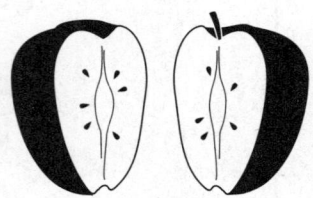

2. Claire ate some pie.
   About how much did
   she eat?
   Circle the answer.

   $\frac{1}{2}$ $\frac{1}{3}$ $\frac{1}{4}$

3. Rico cut a pie into 4 equal
   parts and ate one piece
   of pie.
   What part did he eat?
   Circle the fraction.

   $\frac{1}{2}$ $\frac{1}{3}$ $\frac{1}{4}$

4. Pat bakes pies.
   She gives $\frac{1}{3}$ of the pies to
   a friend.
   Color the part of the pies
   that she gives away.

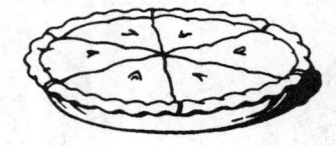

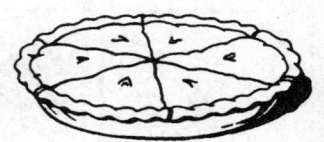

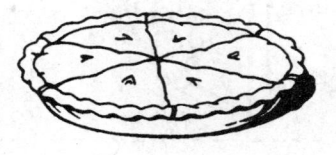

www.harcourtschoolsupply.com
© Harcourt Achieve Inc. All rights reserved.

Lesson 10, Fractions: Word Problems
Math: First Grade, SV 9937-6

Name _____ Date _____

Naming a Pattern

➤ Draw what comes next. Color the part. Write the fraction. What is the rule?

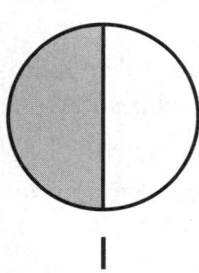

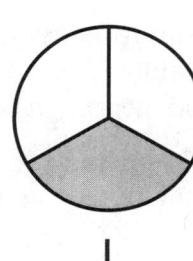

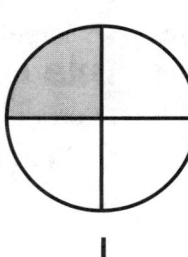

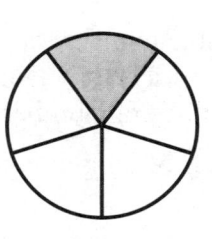

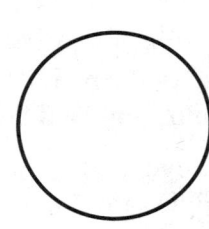

$\frac{1}{2}$ $\frac{1}{3}$ $\frac{1}{4}$ $\frac{1}{5}$ $\frac{}{}$

_____

_____

Name _____ Date _____

Identifying Fraction Clocks

➤ Look at each clock. Draw lines to match the words to the clock.

1.   2.    3.

$\frac{1}{4}$ past the hour $\frac{3}{4}$ past the hour $\frac{1}{2}$ past the hour

www.harcourtschoolsupply.com
© Harcourt Achieve Inc. All rights reserved.

85

Lesson 10, Fractions: Enrichment
Math: First Grade, SV 9937-6

Lesson 11

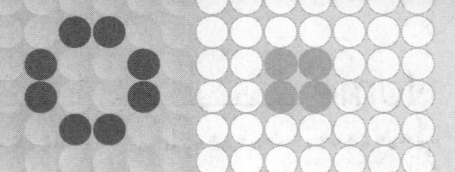

Length

Objectives

- Develop a sense of whole numbers and represent and use them in flexible ways, including relating, composing, and decomposing numbers
- Recognize the attributes of length, volume, weight, area, and time
- Compare and order objects according to these attributes
- Understand how to measure using nonstandard and standard units
- Measure with multiple copies of units of the same size, such as paper clips laid end to end
- Use tools to measure
- Develop common referents for measures to make comparisons and estimates
- Sort and classify objects according to their attributes and organize data about the objects
- Apply and adapt a variety of appropriate strategies to solve problems

Materials

- paper clips, scissors, calendars, books, desks, pencils, inch rulers, centimeter rulers, 3 colors of connecting cubes (optional), container (optional), classroom items to measure (optional), straws (optional), construction paper (optional), yarn (optional), self-sealing plastic bags (optional), dried beans (optional), yardstick (optional)

Lesson Pages

Page 88 (Manipulatives)
Children use paper clips to estimate and measure familiar school items.

Page 89 (Practice)
Children use an inch ruler to measure feathers.

Page 90 (Practice)
Children use a centimeter ruler to measure familiar items.

Page 91 (Extension)
Children use an inch ruler to measure distance on a map.

Page 92 (Word Problems)
Children solve word problems about school tools.

Page 93 (Enrichment)
Activity Card 1: Children write a plan telling how to measure a garden fence without using a yardstick or tape measure.
Activity Card 2: Children use a variety of tools to measure the width of their desks. They record the numbers in a chart.

Another Look

- Put three different colors of connecting cubes in a container. The cubes should be in varying amounts. Invite children to guess which color train will be the longest when the cubes are joined. Have children check their guesses. Finally, ask them to order the trains from smallest to largest. (Visual, Kinesthetic, ELL)

- Cut straws into exact lengths from 1–8 inches. Give partners one length, have them measure it, and find items in the classroom that are about the same length. Have them draw pictures to record their findings. (Visual, Kinesthetic, ELL)

Extension

- Pair children and have them guess the measurement of the length and width of the classroom using their feet (heel to toe) as measuring tools. Then have them check their guesses using a yardstick.

- Cut out paper shapes with exact centimeter measurements. Explain how to find the perimeter by adding the length of the sides. Then challenge children to find the perimeter of the shapes using a centimeter ruler.

At Home

- Cut yarn that is twelve inches long and send it home with the children. Have them measure objects around the house to find things that are about the same length as the yarn ruler. Have them draw pictures to record their findings.

- Give children self-sealing bags that have beans. Ask them to have family members write their first names on paper. Tell children to glue beans end to end on paper to show each letter in the names. Have them compare the names to tell which is longer and which is shorter.

- Visit www.harcourtachieve.com/achievementzone for additional ideas and activity pages.

Answer Key

Page 88
Estimates and measurements will vary.

Page 89
1. 5
2. 1
3. 4
4. 6

Page 90
1. 7
2. 1
3. 3
4. 6

Page 91
1. 4
2. 5
3. 3
4. 2

Page 92
1. Alan; a paper clip is shorter, so more paper clips would be needed.
2. Children draw a line 4 inches long.
3. yes
4. centimeters

Page 93
Card 1: Answers will vary.
Card 2: Answers will vary.

Name _____ Date _____

UNDERSTANDING MEASUREMENT

Clip It

➡ Find these items. About how many 📎 long is each one? Estimate it. Then use 📎 to measure.

	Object	Estimate	Measurement
1.	(scissors)	about _____ 📎	about _____ 📎
2.	(April calendar)	about _____ 📎	about _____ 📎
3.	(book)	about _____ 📎	about _____ 📎
4.	(desk)	about _____ 📎	about _____ 📎

www.harcourtschoolsupply.com
© Harcourt Achieve Inc. All rights reserved.

Lesson 11, Length: Manipulatives
Math: First Grade, SV 9937-6

Name _____ Date _____

MEASURING WITH INCHES

Feather Measure

➤ **How long is each feather? Use an inch ruler.**

1.

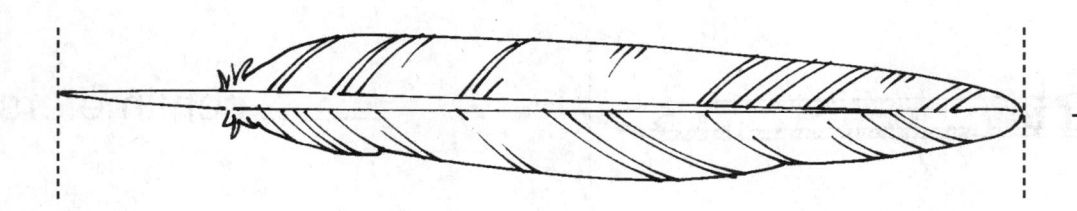

_____ inches

2.

_____ inch

3.

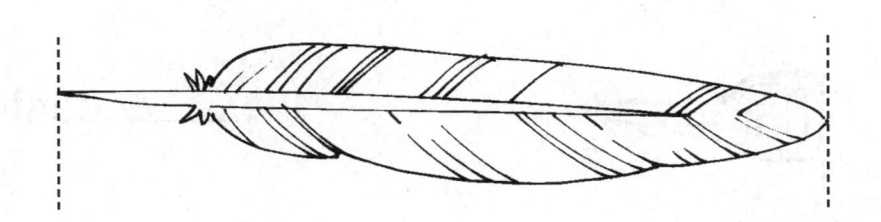

_____ inches

4.

_____ inches

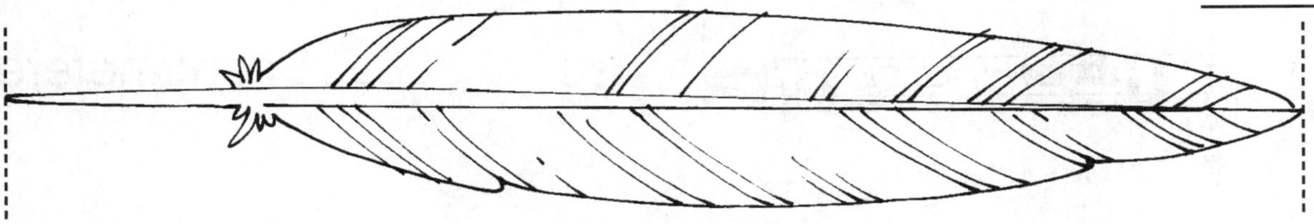

www.harcourtschoolsupply.com
© Harcourt Achieve Inc. All rights reserved.

Lesson 11, Length: Practice
Math: First Grade, SV 9937-6

Name _____ Date _____

MEASURING WITH CENTIMETERS

Measure by Measure

➡ **How long is each object? Use a centimeter ruler.**

1.

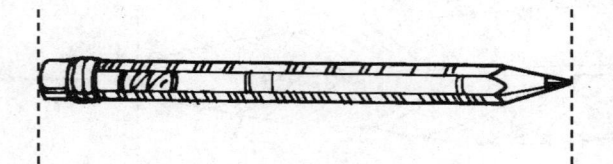

_____ centimeters

2.

_____ centimeter

3.

_____ centimeters

4.

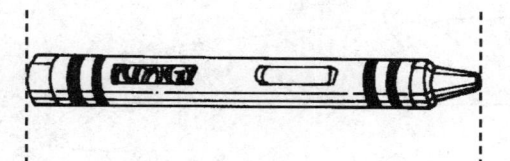

_____ centimeters

www.harcourtschoolsupply.com
© Harcourt Achieve Inc. All rights reserved.

Lesson 11, Length: Practice
Math: First Grade, SV 9937-6

Name _____ Date _____

PRACTICING MEASUREMENT
• •
View the Zoo

➤ **Use an inch ruler. Write how many inches apart.**

1. 🏛 to 🦁 _____ in.   2. 🦁 to 🐘 _____ in.

3. 🐵 to 🦭 _____ in.   4. 🐘 to 🦓 _____ in.

www.harcourtschoolsupply.com
© Harcourt Achieve Inc. All rights reserved.

91

Lesson 11, Length: Extension
Math: First Grade, SV 9937-6

Name _____ Date _____

SOLVING WORD PROBLEMS

School Measuring

➡ **Read each story. Solve.**

1. Rita has a ✏️. Alan has a 📎.
   Who would use more lengths to measure a desk?
   Circle the name. Tell why.

   Rita   Alan

   _____

2. Holly has chalk that is 4 inches long.
   Draw a line to show how long the chalk is.

3. Mark has a pencil box that is 20 centimeters long.
   His pencil is 18 centimeters long.
   Will the pencil fit in the box?
   Circle **yes** or **no**.

   yes   no

4. Lana measures her crayon.
   She writes 10.
   Did Lana measure with inches or centimeters?
   Circle it.

   inches   centimeters

Name _____ Date _____

Planning a Garden

➡ You want to plant a garden. First, you need to build a fence around it. How can you find how much fence you will need without using a yardstick or tape measure? Write your ideas.

Name _____ Date _____

Measuring a Desk

➡ Use each tool. Measure the top of your desk. Write the answer in the chart.

Desk Top

Tool	🖇	inches	centimeters
Desk Length			

Lesson 11, Length: Enrichment
Math: First Grade, SV 9937-6

Lesson 12

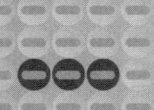

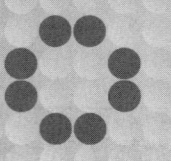

Time

Objectives

- Recognize the attributes of length, volume, weight, area, and time
- Compare and order objects according to these attributes
- Develop common referents for measures to make comparisons and estimates
- Use tools to measure
- Apply and adapt a variety of appropriate strategies to solve problems

Materials

- copies of analog clock on page 128, paper plates, fasteners, glue, scissors, pencils, crayons, masking tape or chalk (optional), index cards (optional), number cards (optional), recycled magazines (optional)

Lesson Pages

Page 96 (Manipulatives)
Duplicate the analog clock parts on page 128. Have children cut out the clock parts and glue the clock face on a paper plate. Show them how to push the fastener through the hands and the plate. After children assemble the clock, have them model times shown on the clocks and write the times.

Page 97 (Practice)
Children circle pictures to show which activity in a pair takes more time.

Page 98 (Practice)
Children learn about time to the half hour by reading digital clock times and drawing the hands on analog clocks.

Page 99 (Extension)
Children estimate how many minutes it will take to complete a dot-to-dot picture. Then they check their guess.

Page 100 (Word Problems)
Children read stories and solve time problems.

Page 101 (Enrichment)
Activity Card 1: Children make a schedule to tell how long it takes to bake a favorite food.
Activity Card 2: Children record the activities they do to get ready for bed and make a time schedule.

Another Look

- Write digital times to the hour and half hour on sets of index cards. Give a set of cards and an analog clock to pairs of children. Have them take turns reading a time that partners show. (Auditory, Kinesthetic, ELL)

- Make a tape circle on the floor or draw a chalk circle outside. Then distribute large cards numbered 1–12. Have children arrange themselves to show a clock face. Ask 2 additional children to be the hour and minute hands on the clock. Name a time to the hour and have children holding those cards repeat "tick tock." The "hands" point to the appropriate number, too. Repeat the activity so that each child can participate. (Visual, Kinesthetic, Auditory, ELL)

Extension

- Display a class schedule on the chalkboard and discuss it with children. Assign daily "clock watchers" to make sure the class stays on time.

- Invite children to cut out pictures of familiar activities, such as eating or sleeping, from recycled magazines. Have children write the time that someone might do the activity. Then have children work in small groups to order their pictures from morning to night. Repeat the activity several times.

At Home

- Tell children to choose one favorite television program and find out what time it starts and ends. Ask them to draw pictures of the clock to show what the hands look like when the program starts and ends. Have them write the time at school the next day.

- Suggest that children talk with family members about the time they do specific activities, such as get up in the morning, eat dinner, or attend extracurricular events. Encourage them to draw clock faces to show the times.

- Visit www.harcourtachieve.com/achievementzone for additional ideas and activity pages.

Answer Key

Page 96
1. 3
2. 7
3. 8
4. 5
5. 9
6. 1
7. 12
8. 4

Page 97
Children circle the following pictures:
1. boy reading thick book
2. man drying many dishes
3. girl painting the wall
4. the 100 piece puzzle

Page 98
Children draw hands to show the times on the digital clocks.

Page 99
Answers will vary.

Page 100
1. 5
2. Children draw hands to show 4:30.
3. 6:00
4. Children circle the football helmet.

Page 101
Card 1: Answers will vary.
Card 2: Answers will vary.

Name _____ Date _____

UNDERSTANDING TIME TO THE HOUR
....

"Hour" Clock

➡ **Show the time on the clock. Write the time.**

1. ___:00

2. ___:00

3. ___:00

4. ___:00

5. ___:00

6. ___:00

7. ___:00

8. ___:00

www.harcourtschoolsupply.com
© Harcourt Achieve Inc. All rights reserved.

96

Lesson 12, Time: Manipulatives
Math: First Grade, SV 9937-6

Name _____   Date _____

ESTIMATING TIME
....

How Long?

➡ Which takes more time? Circle it.

1.

2.

3.

4.

www.harcourtschoolsupply.com
© Harcourt Achieve Inc. All rights reserved.

97

Lesson 12, Time: Practice
Math: First Grade, SV 9937-6

Name _____ Date _____

WRITING TIME TO THE HALF HOUR
•••

Hands On

➧ **Draw hands on the clock to show each time.**

1. 2:30

2. 10:30

3. 7:30

4. 6:30

5. 12:30

6. 4:30

Name _____ Date _____

ESTIMATING TIME TO THE MINUTE
••

Dot-to-Dot Time

➤ Estimate how many minutes you think it will take to complete the picture. Use a clock to time how long it takes.

Estimate　　　　　　　　　　　**My time**

____ minutes　　　　　　　　　　____ minutes

www.harcourtschoolsupply.com
© Harcourt Achieve Inc. All rights reserved.

99

Lesson 12, Time: Extension
Math: First Grade, SV 9937-6

Name _____   Date _____

SOLVING WORD PROBLEMS
....

Game Time

➡ **Read each story. Solve.**

1. Brad has a baseball game.
What time is the game?
Write the time.

____:00

2. The time on Lina's clock was wrong.
She missed soccer practice.
Draw hands to show what the clock should look like.

4:30

3. Ana starts basketball practice at 4:00.
It lasts 2 hours.
What time is practice over?
Write the time.

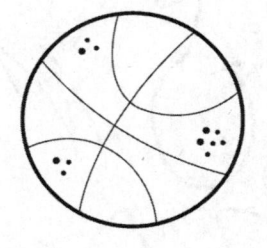

_____

4. Marcos plays baseball and football.
Which hat takes more time to put on?
Circle it.

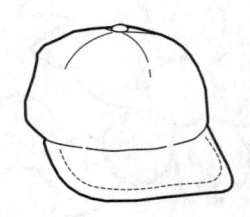

www.harcourtschoolsupply.com
© Harcourt Achieve Inc. All rights reserved.

100

Lesson 12, Time: Word Problems
Math: First Grade, SV 9937-6

Name _____   Date _____

Baking Time

➡ What is your favorite food? Write a time schedule to show how long it takes to make and bake it. Draw a picture of your food on another sheet of paper.

Activity	Time

Name _____   Date _____

Going to Bed

➡ What must you do before going to bed each night? How long do you think each activity takes? Write a schedule.

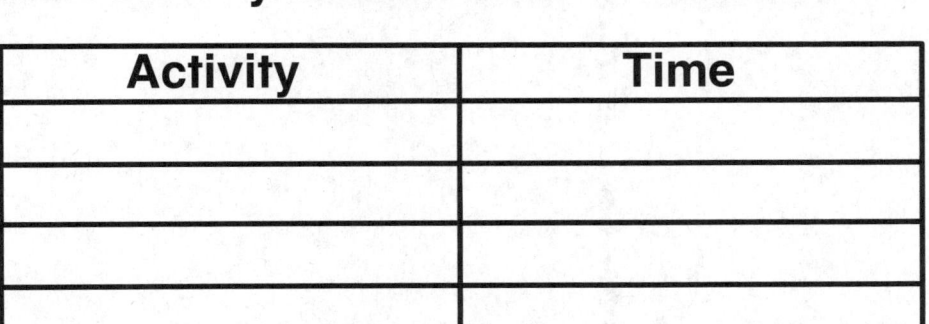

Activity	Time

www.harcourtschoolsupply.com
© Harcourt Achieve Inc. All rights reserved.

Lesson 12, Time: Enrichment
Math: First Grade, SV 9937-6

Lesson 13

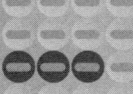

Money

Objectives

- Count with understanding and recognize "how many" in sets of objects
- Develop a sense of whole numbers and represent and use them in flexible ways, including relating, composing, and decomposing numbers
- Connect number words and numerals to the quantities they represent, using various physical models and representations
- Use a variety of methods and tools to compute, including objects, mental computation, estimation, paper and pencil, and calculators
- Develop common referents for measures to make comparisons and estimates
- Apply and adapt a variety of appropriate strategies to solve problems

Materials

- coin manipulatives, pencils, crayons, envelopes (optional), toy pictures from recycled magazines and newspaper ads (optional), price tags (optional), plastic cups (optional)

Lesson Pages

Page 104 (Manipulatives)
Children use coin manipulatives to identify a penny, nickel, dime, and quarter and write the value of each.

Page 105 (Practice)
Children circle the coins needed to buy fruit.

Page 106 (Practice)
Using the count-on strategy, children find the value of sets of coins.

Page 107 (Extension)
Children find the path through a maze and add the values of coins along the path.

Page 108 (Word Problems)
Children solve word problems about money.

Page 109 (Enrichment)
Activity Card 1: Children get a handful of coins and find the value. Then they trade to find the least number of coins they can have to equal that value.
Activity Card 2: Children make a list to show 3 ways they can spend $1.00 at a bake sale.

Another Look

- Show each kind of coin. Have children count out the number of pennies to show the amount. (Visual, Kinesthetic, ELL)

- Place a variety of coins in envelopes. Write the values of the coins on separate cards. Then invite partners to choose an envelope, count the coins, and choose the correct card. While sorting the coins, have partners look at and describe the coins according to color, size, pictures, and numbers they see. (Visual, Auditory)

Extension

- Cut out toy pictures from recycled magazines or newspaper ads. Make price tags up to 99¢ to glue to them. Then have children get a handful of coins. Have them count the coins and "shop" for the items they will buy.

- Put different amounts of coins in plastic cups. Have children trade coins to show the least number of coins for a value.

At Home

- Suggest that children go shopping with a family member. Challenge them to count out the coins needed to pay for the cents part of the price.

- Suggest that children ask family members for the coins they have in a pocket or purse. Ask them to use the count-on strategy to find the total value of the coins.

- Visit www.harcourtachieve.com/achievementzone for additional ideas and activity pages.

Answer Key

Page 104
1. penny; 1
2. quarter; 25
3. dime; 10
4. nickel; 5

Page 105
Children circle:
1. 7 pennies
2. 9 pennies
3. 1 nickel
4. 5 nickels

Page 106
1. 25, 30, 31, 32; 32¢
2. 25, 35, 45, 50; 50¢
3. 25, 35, 40, 45, 46; 46¢
4. 25, 35, 45, 50, 55, 56; 56¢

Page 107
Children follow this path: quarter, dime, dime, nickel, penny, penny.
The value is 52¢.

Page 108
1. yes
2. Jan
3. 25¢
4. Children circle 1 quarter.

Page 109
Card 1: Answers will vary.
Card 2: Answers will vary.

Name _____ Date _____

IDENTIFYING COINS

Feed the Bank

➡ Show the coin for each amount. Then draw the coin. Write how many cents.

1.

1 cent

_____ ¢

2.

25 cents

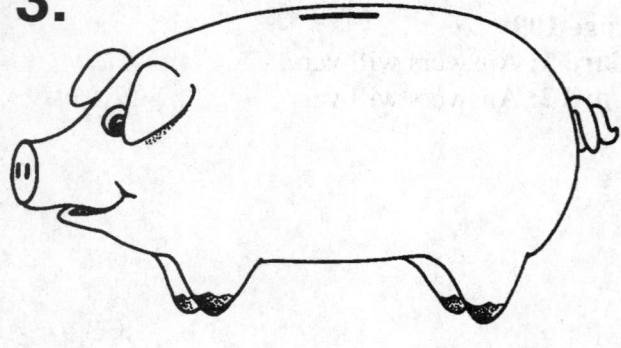

_____ ¢

3.

10 cents

_____ ¢

4.

5 cents

_____ ¢

www.harcourtschoolsupply.com
© Harcourt Achieve Inc. All rights reserved.

104

Lesson 13, Money: Manipulatives
Math: First Grade, SV 9937-6

Name _____ Date _____

COUNTING PENNIES AND NICKELS

Fruit Cents

➤ Circle how much money is needed.

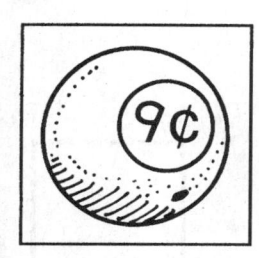

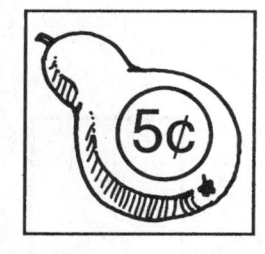

1. 7¢

2. 9¢

3. 5¢

4. 25¢

www.harcourtschoolsupply.com
© Harcourt Achieve Inc. All rights reserved.

Lesson 13, Money: Practice
Math: First Grade, SV 9937-6

Name _____ Date _____

COUNTING ON
....

Coin Count

➡ **Count on. Write the amount.**

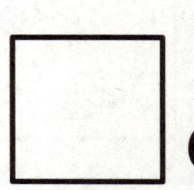

1. ___¢ ___¢ ___¢ ___¢   ☐ ¢

2. ___¢ ___¢ ___¢ ___¢   ☐ ¢

3. ___¢ ___¢ ___¢ ___¢ ___¢   ☐ ¢

4. ___¢ ___¢ ___¢ ___¢ ___¢ ___¢   ☐ ¢

www.harcourtschoolsupply.com
© Harcourt Achieve Inc. All rights reserved.

106

Lesson 13, Money: Practice
Math: First Grade, SV 9937-6

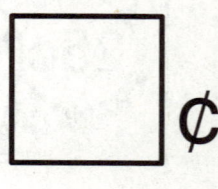

Name _____ Date _____

COUNTING COINS

Cool Buys

➡ **The children are going to buy ice cream. Draw a line to show the way. Start with the quarter. Then count the coins to find how much money they have.**

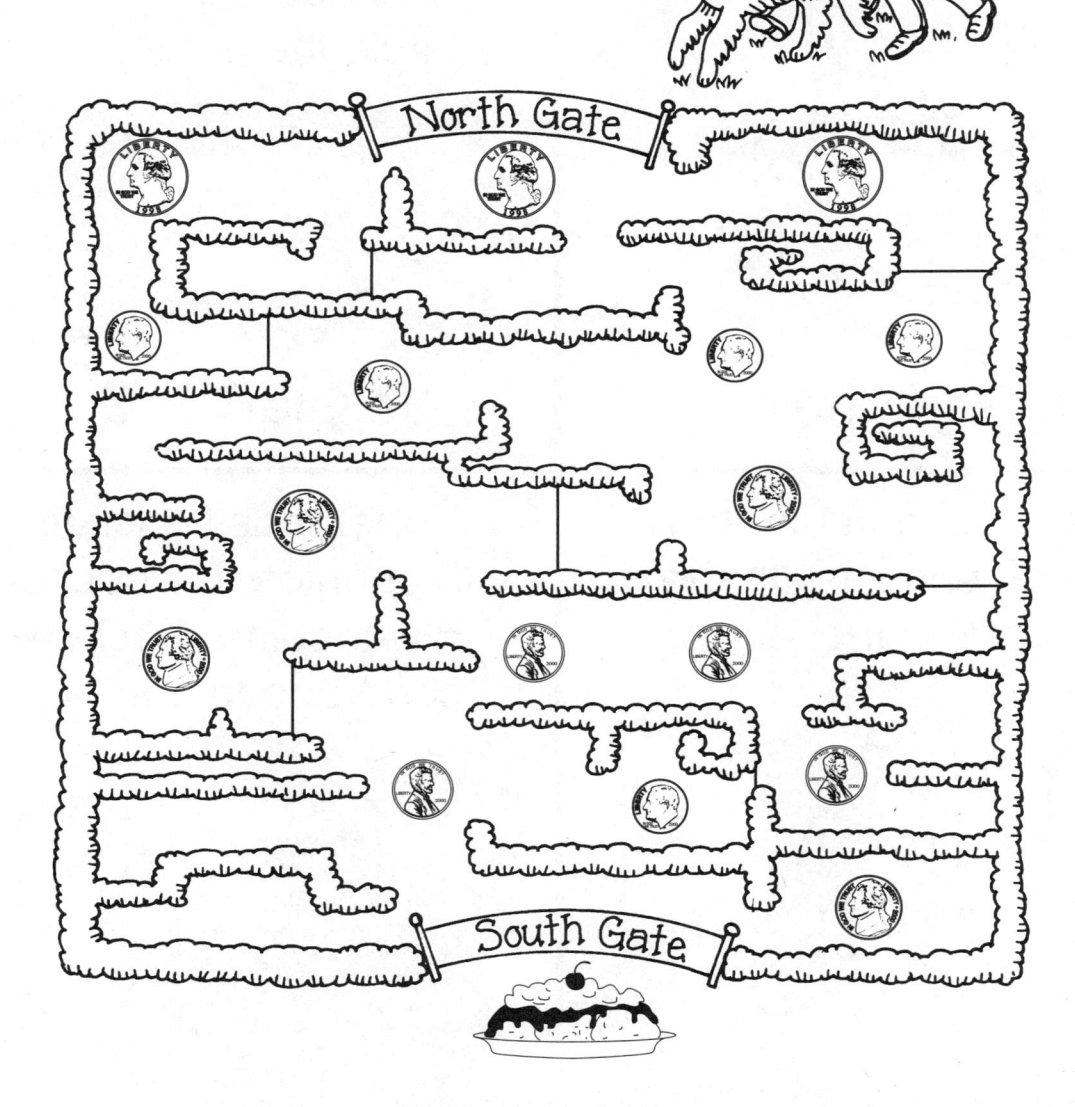

The children have _____ ¢.

www.harcourtschoolsupply.com
© Harcourt Achieve Inc. All rights reserved.

107

Lesson 13, Money: Extension
Math: First Grade, SV 9937-6

Name _____ Date _____

SOLVING WORD PROBLEMS

The Problem with Money

➡ Read each problem. Solve.

1. Greg has 2 nickels.
Can he buy the apple?
Circle **yes** or **no**.

9¢

yes   no

2. Jessie has 2 dimes and
1 nickel. Jan has 1 quarter
and 3 pennies.
Who has more?
Circle the name.

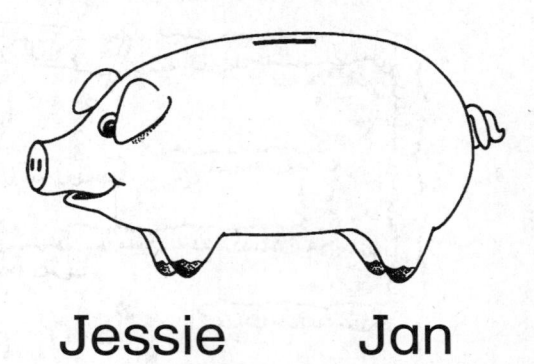

Jessie   Jan

3. Circle the amount that
can be shown with the
least number of coins.

15¢   20¢   25¢

4. Robert has 4 nickels and
5 pennies. He trades to get
fewer coins. Circle what he
can trade to get.

www.harcourtschoolsupply.com
© Harcourt Achieve Inc. All rights reserved.

108

Lesson 13, Money: Word Problems
Math: First Grade, SV 9937-6

Name _____ Date _____

Trading Coins

➥ Get a handful of coins. How much do you have? Write the amount. Trade the coins to get the least number of coins for that amount.

I have ____ ¢.

Name _____ Date _____

Buying at a Bake Sale

➥ You have $1.00. What will you buy? List 3 ways you can spend the money.

32¢   40¢   77¢   58¢

1. _____
2. _____
3. _____

www.harcourtschoolsupply.com
© Harcourt Achieve Inc. All rights reserved.

109

Lesson 13, Money: Enrichment
Math: First Grade, SV 9937-6

Lesson 14

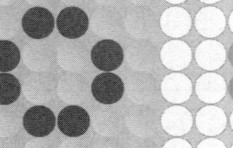

Graphs

Objectives

- Count with understanding and recognize "how many" in sets of objects
- Develop a sense of whole numbers and represent and use them in flexible ways, including relating, composing, and decomposing numbers
- Pose questions and gather data about themselves and their surroundings
- Sort and classify objects according to their attributes and organize data about the objects
- Represent data using concrete objects, pictures, and graphs
- Describe parts of the data and the set of data as a whole to determine what the data show
- Apply and adapt a variety of appropriate strategies to solve problems

Materials

- red, blue, and yellow connecting cubes; crayons; pencils; 1-inch graph paper; construction paper in a variety of colors (optional); pattern blocks (optional); chart paper (optional); craft paper (optional); markers or paint (optional); self-sealing plastic bags (optional); dried beans (optional)

Lesson Pages

Page 112 (Manipulatives)
To develop an understanding of bar graphs, children use connecting cubes to count colors of balloons in a picture.

Page 113 (Practice)
Children count shapes and color the boxes to complete a graph.

Page 114 (Practice)
Children answer questions about a bar graph.

Page 115 (Extension)
Children look at a picture and complete a bar graph to show the animals in a pet shop.

Page 116 (Word Problems)
Children solve word problems about a graph.

Page 117 (Enrichment)
Activity Card 1: Children poll classmates and make a graph about favorite ice cream.
Activity Card 2: Children look at a picture of toy vehicles. They find one way to sort them and make a graph to show the results. Then they write three questions for a friend to answer.

Another Look

- Have partners get a handful of different colors of connecting cubes. Tell them to make trains with cubes that are the same color. Have them align the left ends of the trains. Ask questions that help children understand how the cubes make a graph. (Visual, Auditory, ELL)

- Lay out a variety of colors of construction paper. Invite each child to choose a favorite color of paper and write his or her name on it. Help children create a large graph on the floor, showing favorite colors. Discuss the importance of a title and the scale as you add it to the graph. (Visual, Kinesthetic, ELL)

Extension

- Invite partners to make a picture or a design with pattern blocks. Have them sort the blocks and draw a graph on 1-inch graph paper showing the groups. Challenge partners to take turns asking questions about the graph.

- Draw a graph on chart paper showing a frog with 3 squares colored, a duck with 6 squares colored, a fish with 4 squares colored, and a turtle with 2 squares colored. Invite groups of children to make a mural of a pond scene on craft paper showing the number of animals.

At Home

- In advance, purchase a bag of mixed dried beans. Put a small amount of beans in self-sealing plastic bags. Send the beans home with children. Tell them to make a pictograph using the beans.

- Give each child a sheet of 1-inch graph paper. Write the color names on the board and ask children to use them as category names to make a graph on the paper. Tell them to take the graph home and ask family members to color a block for their favorite color. Suggest a family member ask questions about the graph for children to answer.

- Visit www.harcourtachieve.com/achievementzone for additional ideas and activity pages.

Answer Key

Page 112
Children color boxes to show:
red–4
yellow–2
blue–5

Page 113
Children color boxes to show:
triangles–8
squares–4
circles–7
rectangles–5

Page 114
1. 5
2. dogs
3. birds and fish
4. 8

Page 115
Children color boxes to show:
dogs–4
cats–4
fish–6
birds–2

Page 116
1. ||||| |
2. 4 + 5 = 9
3. 3 − 1 = 2

Page 117
Card 1: Answers will vary.
Card 2: Answers will vary.

Name _____ Date _____

UNDERSTANDING A GRAPH

Clowning Around with Graphs

▶ Put a cube on each balloon to show the color. Join cubes that are the same color. Color a square in the graph for each color.

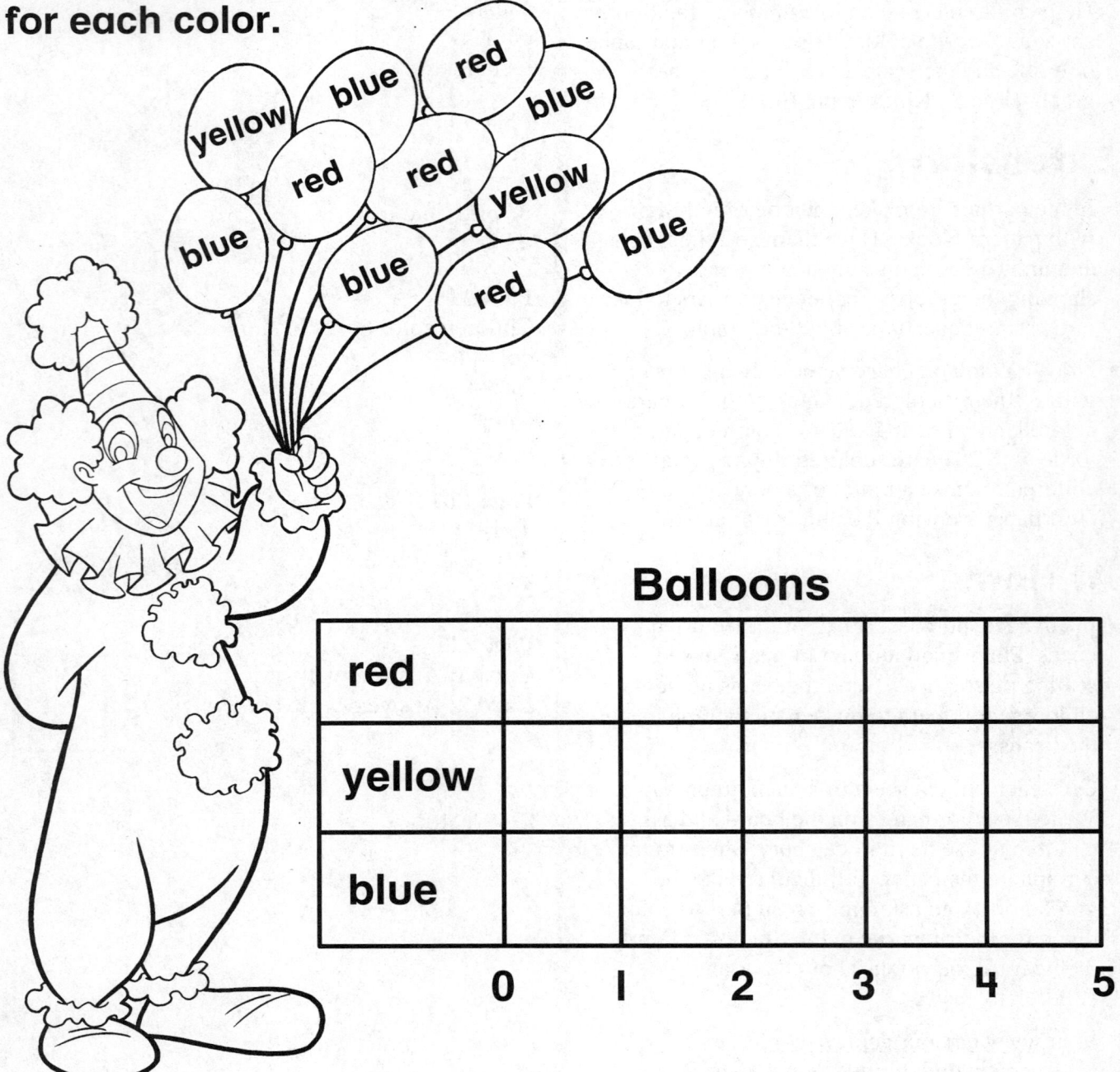

Balloons on clown: yellow, blue, red, blue, red, red, red, blue, blue, yellow, red, blue

Balloons

red					
yellow					
blue					

0   1   2   3   4   5

www.harcourtschoolsupply.com
© Harcourt Achieve Inc. All rights reserved.

112

Lesson 14, Graphs: Manipulatives
Math: First Grade, SV 9937-6

Name _____ Date _____

MAKING A GRAPH
....

Shape Sort

➡ **Count the shapes. Complete the graph.**

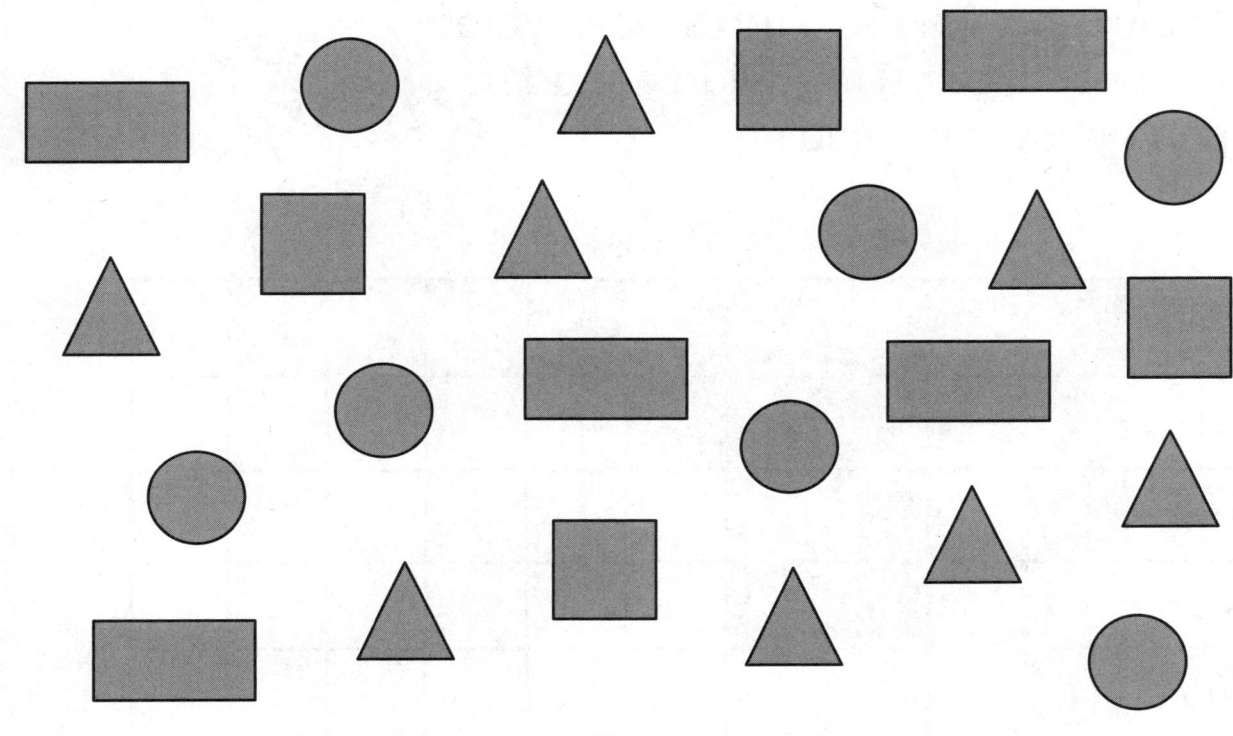

Shapes

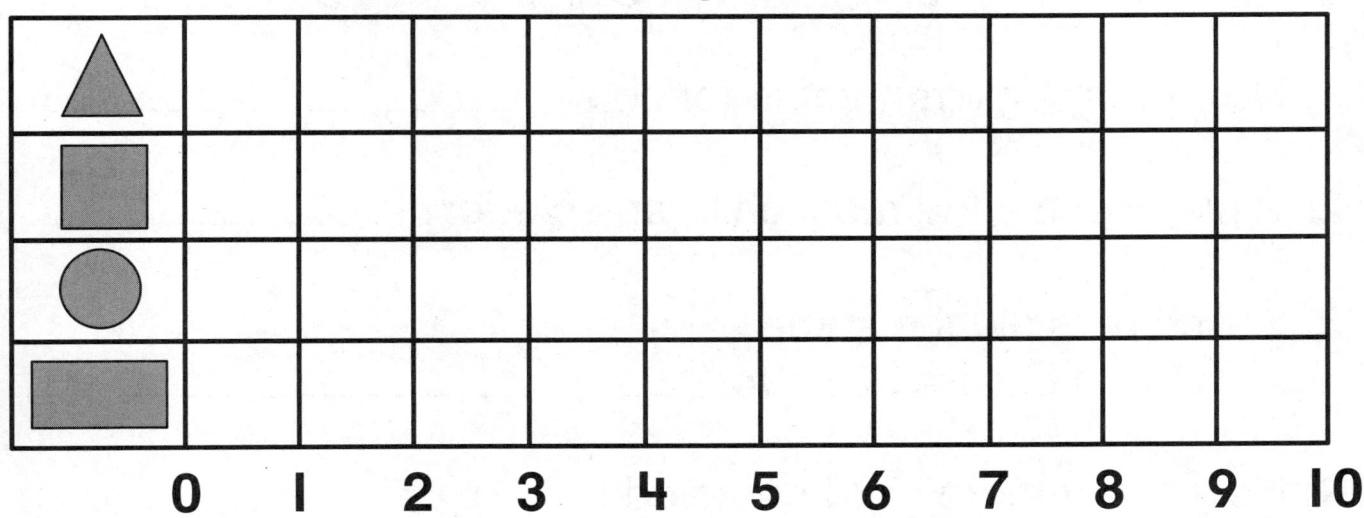

	0	1	2	3	4	5	6	7	8	9	10
△											
▪											
●											
▬											

www.harcourtschoolsupply.com
© Harcourt Achieve Inc. All rights reserved.

Lesson 14, Graphs: Practice
Math: First Grade, SV 9937-6

Name _____ Date _____

READING A GRAPH
....

Favorite Pets

➡ **Look at the graph. Then answer the questions.**

The 23 students in Miss Tran's class voted for their favorite pet. The children made a graph to show their findings.

Pets

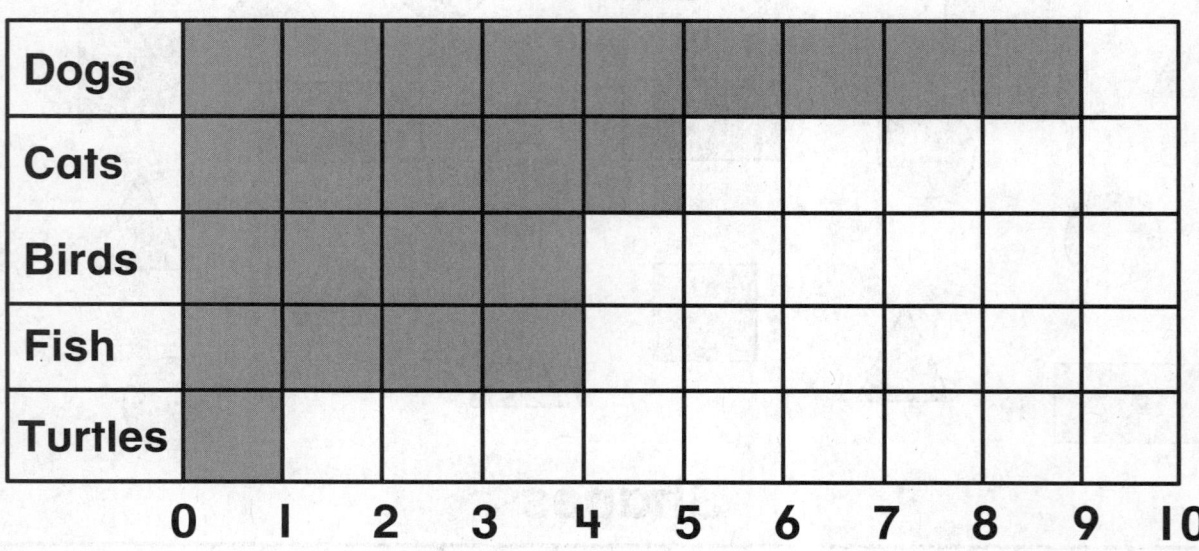

	0	1	2	3	4	5	6	7	8	9	10
Dogs											
Cats											
Birds											
Fish											
Turtles											

1. How many children voted for cats? _____

2. Which pet did the most children vote for? _____

3. Which pets did the same number of children vote for? _____

4. How many more children voted for dogs than voted for turtles? _____

www.harcourtschoolsupply.com
© Harcourt Achieve Inc. All rights reserved.

114

Lesson 14, Graphs: Practice
Math: First Grade, SV 9937-6

Name _____ Date _____

PRACTICING GRAPHING SKILLS
Picture This Graph

➥ **Color the picture. Then complete the graph to show the animals in a pet shop.**

Animals in a Pet Shop

Dogs							
Cats							
Fish							
Birds							

0   1   2   3   4   5   6

www.harcourtschoolsupply.com
© Harcourt Achieve Inc. All rights reserved.

Lesson 14, Graphs: Extension
Math: First Grade, SV 9937-6

Name _____ Date _____

SOLVING WORD PROBLEMS

Nursery Rhyme Favorites

➡ **Look at the graph. Read each story. Then answer the questions.**

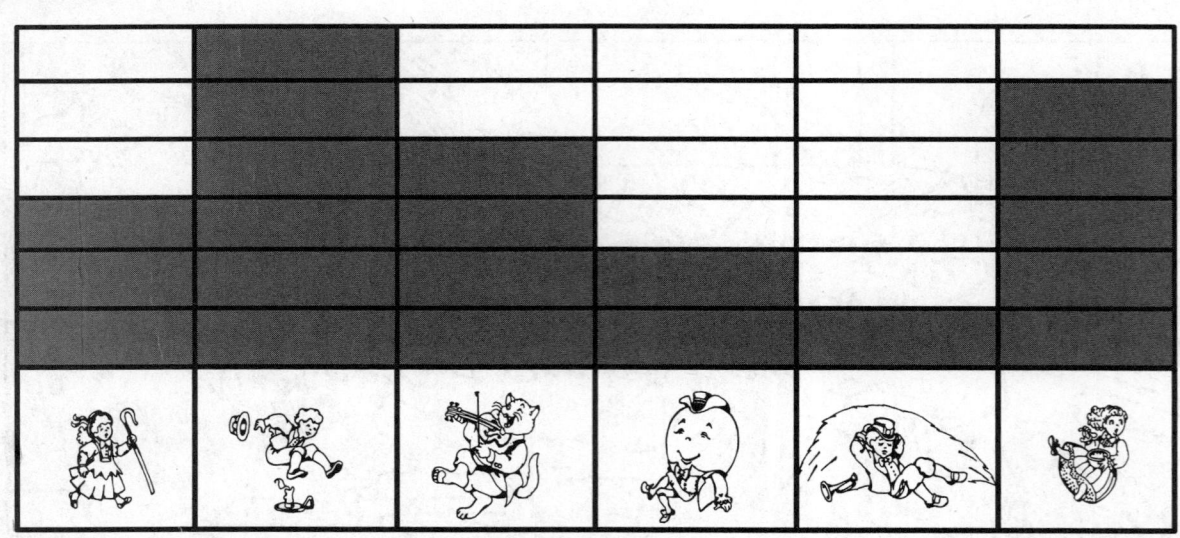

1. Jill made the graph. She asked friends to vote for their favorite nursery rhymes.
   How would she show the votes of people who like 🧒 ?
   Write the tally marks in the box. ☐

2. Jill wanted to know how many voted for 🐱 and 👧 . 
   What number sentence did Jill write?
   Write it on the line. _____

3. Jill wanted to know how many more voted for 👧 than 🧒 . 
   What number sentence did Jill write?
   Write it on the line. _____

Name _____ Date _____

Asking and Graphing

➡ What kind of ice cream do most of your friends like? Ask 10 people. Make a tally mark for each vote. Then make a graph to show the votes.

Flavor	Votes

Name _____ Date _____

Making a Graph

➡ Sort the toys. Make a graph to show how many of each. Write 3 questions about the graph. Give the graph and the questions to a friend to answer.

www.harcourtschoolsupply.com
© Harcourt Achieve Inc. All rights reserved.

Lesson 14, Graphs: Enrichment
Math: First Grade, SV 9937-6

Lesson 15

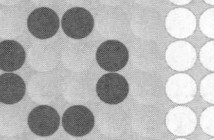

Probability

Objectives

- Sort and classify objects according to their attributes and organize data about the objects
- Represent data using concrete objects, pictures, and graphs
- Describe parts of the data and the set of data as a whole to determine what the data show
- Discuss events related to students' experiences as likely or unlikely
- Apply and adapt a variety of appropriate strategies to solve problems

Materials

- red and yellow bi-colored counters, pencils, crayons, color tiles, sacks, connecting cubes (optional), construction paper (optional), realistic fiction and fantasy books (optional), copies of circles (optional), paper clips (optional)

Lesson Pages

Page 120 (Manipulatives)
To develop an understanding of probability, children toss a 2-sided counter and record the results in charts.

Page 121 (Practice)
Children place 4 red and 4 blue tiles in a sack. Partners take turns pulling tiles and recording the colors they get.

Page 122 (Practice)
Children repeat the game from page 121 but use 5 blue tiles and 1 red tile.

Page 123 (Extension)
Partners simultaneously draw paths, one straight and one zigzag, to see which is more likely the faster way to get to a park.

Page 124 (Word Problems)
Children solve word problems to show an understanding of probability.

Page 125 (Enrichment)
Activity Card 1: Children explore probability using three variables.
Activity Card 2: Children explore how to make a fair game board that is divided into 4 parts.

Another Look

- Join connecting cubes to make 8 pattern trains. Put them on separate pieces of construction paper. Add 2 more cubes to each construction paper, one of which will come next in the pattern. Have children add the cube that will most likely come next. (Visual, Kinesthetic, ELL)

- Gather a variety of books. Some have events that could happen and some have events that could not happen. Have children sort the books into likely and unlikely stories. (Visual, Kinesthetic)

Extension

- Have children repeat the Tile Game on page 121, but have children use 3 colors of tiles. In advance, discuss how the probability changes.

- Provide copies of circles. Challenge children to create a game with a spinner that is fair.

At Home

- Have children explain the Tile Game on page 121 to a family member. Suggest they play the game at home using paper squares of the same colors.

- Ask children to invite a family member to predict if more heads or tails will come up on a coin toss. Then have children challenge the person to check the guess.

- Visit www.harcourtachieve.com/achievementzone for additional ideas and activity pages.

Answer Key

Page 120
Answers will vary.

Page 121
Answers will vary.

Page 122
Answers will vary.

Page 123
Children will color the straight path.

Page 124
1. Robyn
2. 4
3. 2
4. can't tell

Page 125
Card 1: 3 triangles, 2 triangles and 1 circle, 1 triangle and 2 circles, and 3 circles
Card 2:

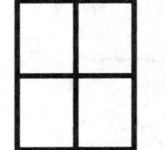

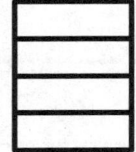

Name _____ Date _____

UNDERSTANDING PROBABILITY
Color Toss

1. Get a counter that is red on 1 side and yellow on 1 side. Toss the counter 10 times. Mark in the table to tell the color that shows each time.

Red	
Yellow	

2. Toss the counter 10 more times. Mark in the table to tell the color that shows each time.

Red	
Yellow	

3. Look at the first 2 charts. What do you think might happen if you toss the counter 10 more times? Mark your guesses in the chart.

Red	
Yellow	

4. Now toss the counter 10 more times. Fill in the chart. Is it close to your guesses? _____

Red	
Yellow	

www.harcourtschoolsupply.com
© Harcourt Achieve Inc. All rights reserved.

Lesson 15, Probability: Manipulatives
Math: First Grade, SV 9937-6

Name _____ Date _____

EXPLORING PROBABILITY

The Tile Game

➡ **Work with a friend. Play a game. Put 4 blue tiles and 4 red tiles in a bag. Choose red or blue. Your friend gets the other color. Write your names on the chart. Take turns. Pull a tile without looking. Write in the chart the color you get. Tell how many of your color you get in all.**

Name	
Color	

1	
2	
3	
4	
5	
6	
7	
8	
9	
10	

How many? _____

Name	
Color	

1	
2	
3	
4	
5	
6	
7	
8	
9	
10	

How many? _____

Name _____ Date _____

EXPLORING FAIR GAMES
....

Not Fair!

➤ **Work with a friend. Play a game. Put 5 blue tiles and 1 red tile in a bag. Choose red or blue. Your friend gets the other color. Write your names on the chart. Take turns. Pull a tile without looking. Write in the chart the color you get. Tell how many of your color you get in all.**

Name		Name	
Color		Color	

1		1	
2		2	
3		3	
4		4	
5		5	
6		6	
7		7	
8		8	
9		9	
10		10	

How many? How many?

_____ _____

Is this game fair?   yes   no

www.harcourtschoolsupply.com
© Harcourt Achieve Inc. All rights reserved.

Lesson 15, Probability: Practice
Math: First Grade, SV 9937-6

Name _____   Date _____

EXPLORING LIKELY AND UNLIKELY
....

Hurry to the Park

➡ Look at the map. What is the faster path to the park? Make a guess. Circle **straight** or **zigzag**.

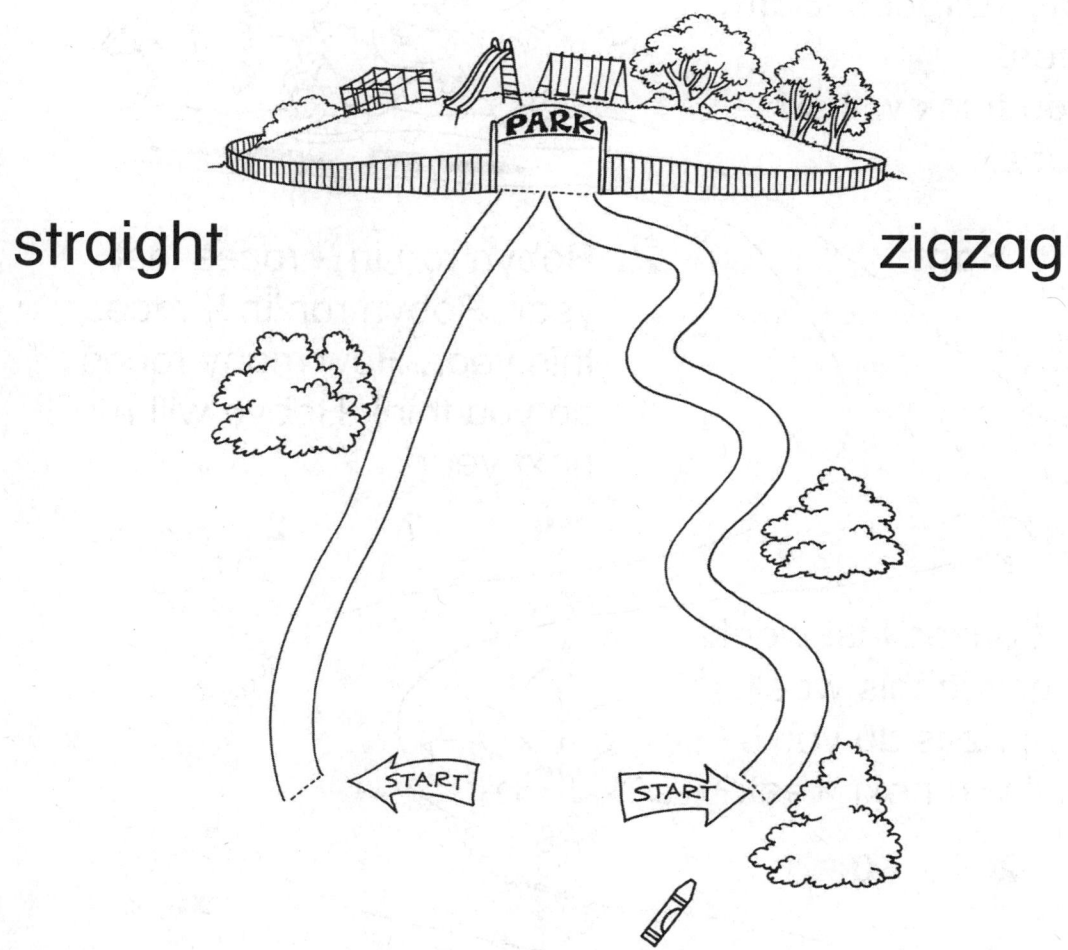

straight   zigzag

Work with a partner. Who will trace the straight path? Who will trace the zigzag path?
Begin at the same time as your partner and trace the path. Then answer the question.

Which path is the faster way to the park? Color the path red.

www.harcourtschoolsupply.com
© Harcourt Achieve Inc. All rights reserved.

Lesson 15, Probability: Extension
Math: First Grade, SV 9937-6

Name _____ Date _____

SOLVING WORD PROBLEMS
....

Take a Guess

➤ Read each story. Circle the answer.

1. Robyn wins 10 races. Sam wins 2 races.
Who do you think will win the next race?

Robyn   **Sam**

2. Robyn ran in 4 races last year. Robyn ran in 4 races this year. How many races do you think Robyn will run next year?

4   7   2

3. Sam won 2 prizes last week. He won 2 prizes this week. How many prizes do you think he will win next week?

5   2   10

4. Robyn's school wins 5 races. Sam's school wins 5 races. Which school do you think will win the next race?

**Robyn's school   Sam's school
can't tell**

Name _____ Date _____

Choosing Shapes

➤ Think about 3 cards. Each has a △ on 1 side. Each has a ○ on the other side. Draw all the ways the cards can land if you let them fall out of a bag.

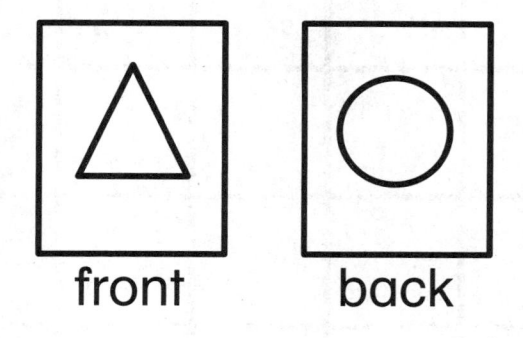

front   back

Name _____ Date _____

Making a Game

➤ Ed wants to make a game. He wants it to be fair. Show 4 ways that Ed can draw the game board so it has 4 equal parts.

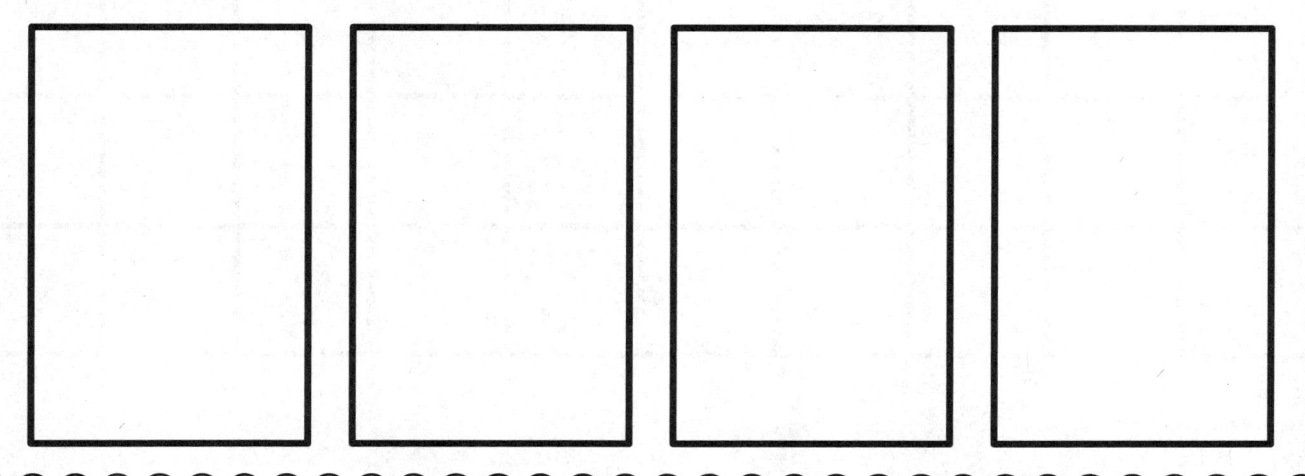

Name _____ Date _____

100 Chart

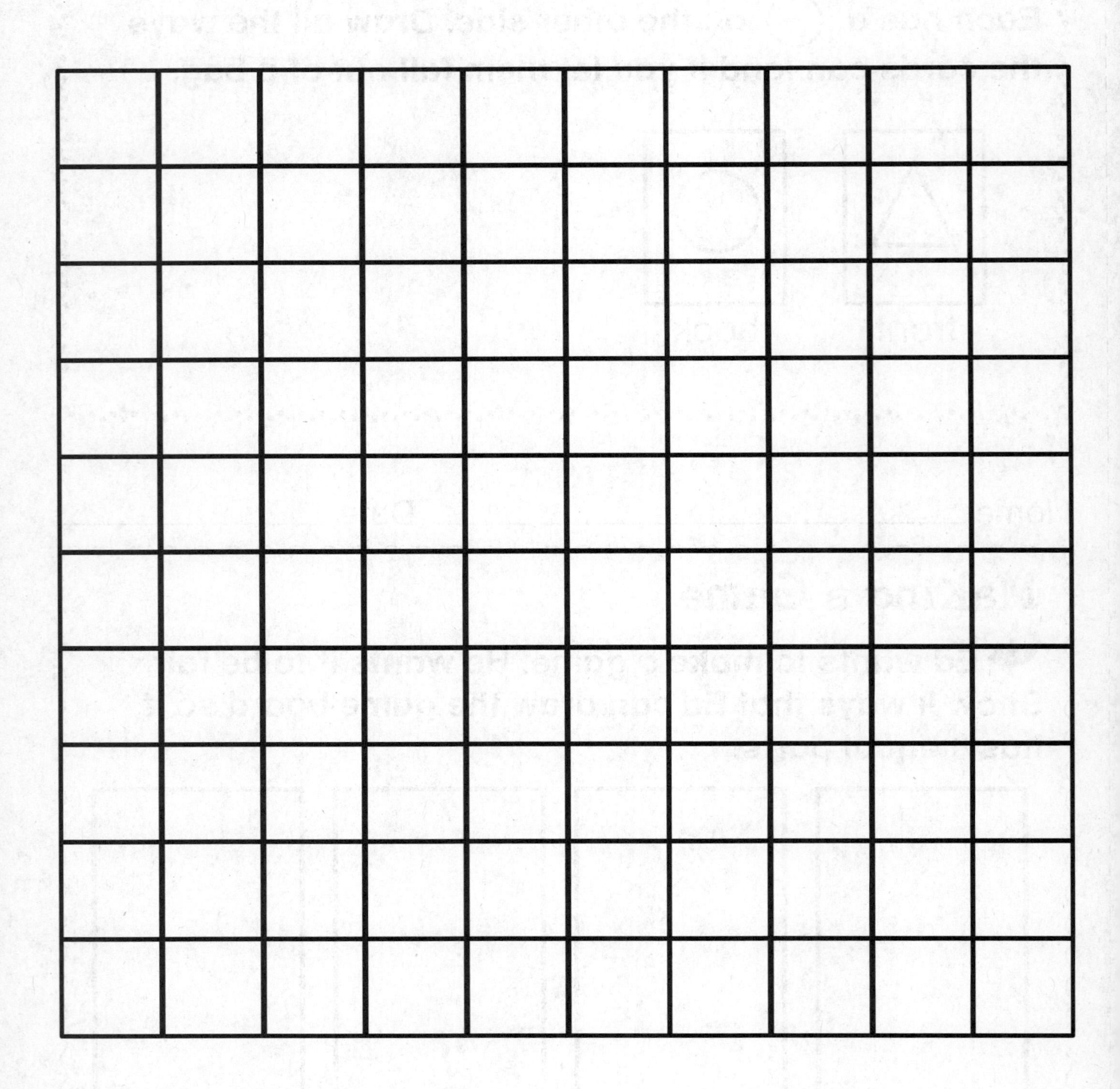

Name _____ Date _____

Shapes

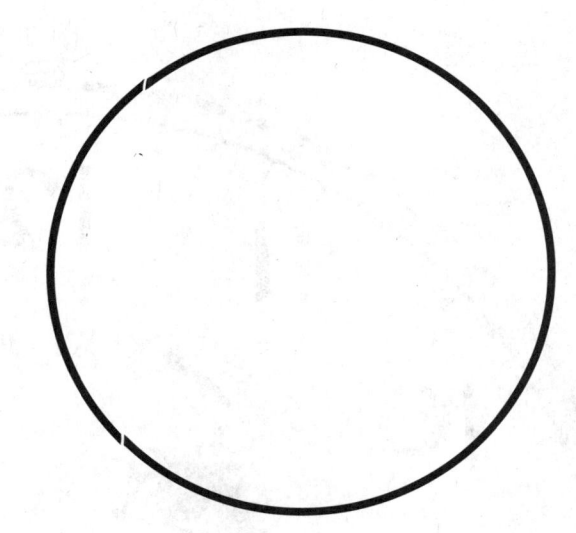

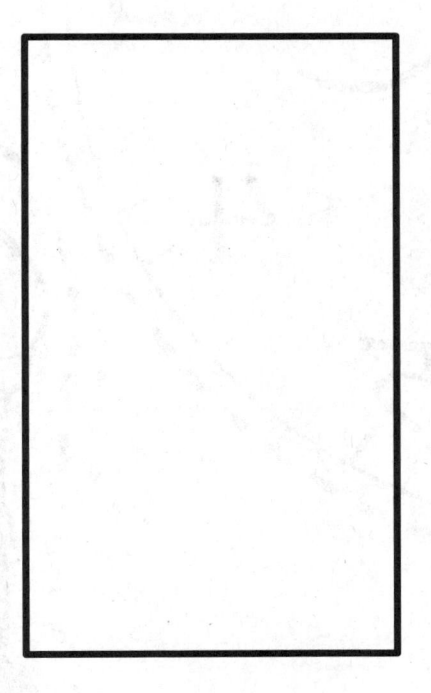

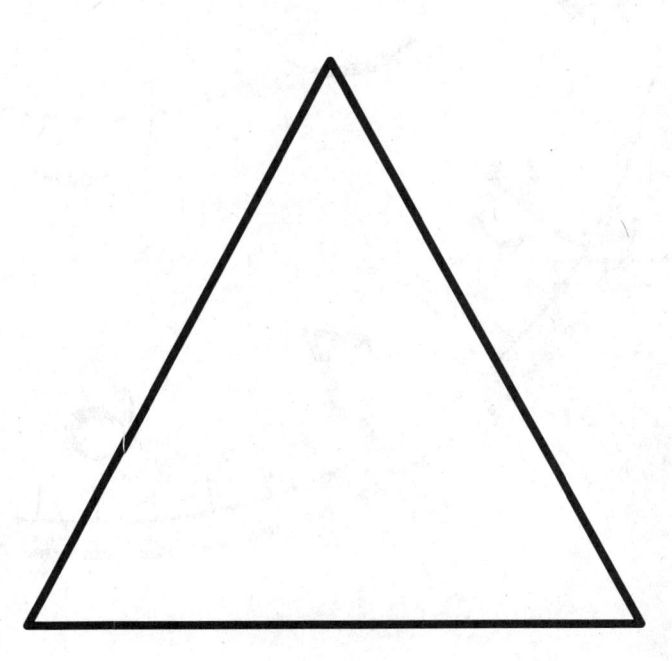

Name _____ Date _____

Clock

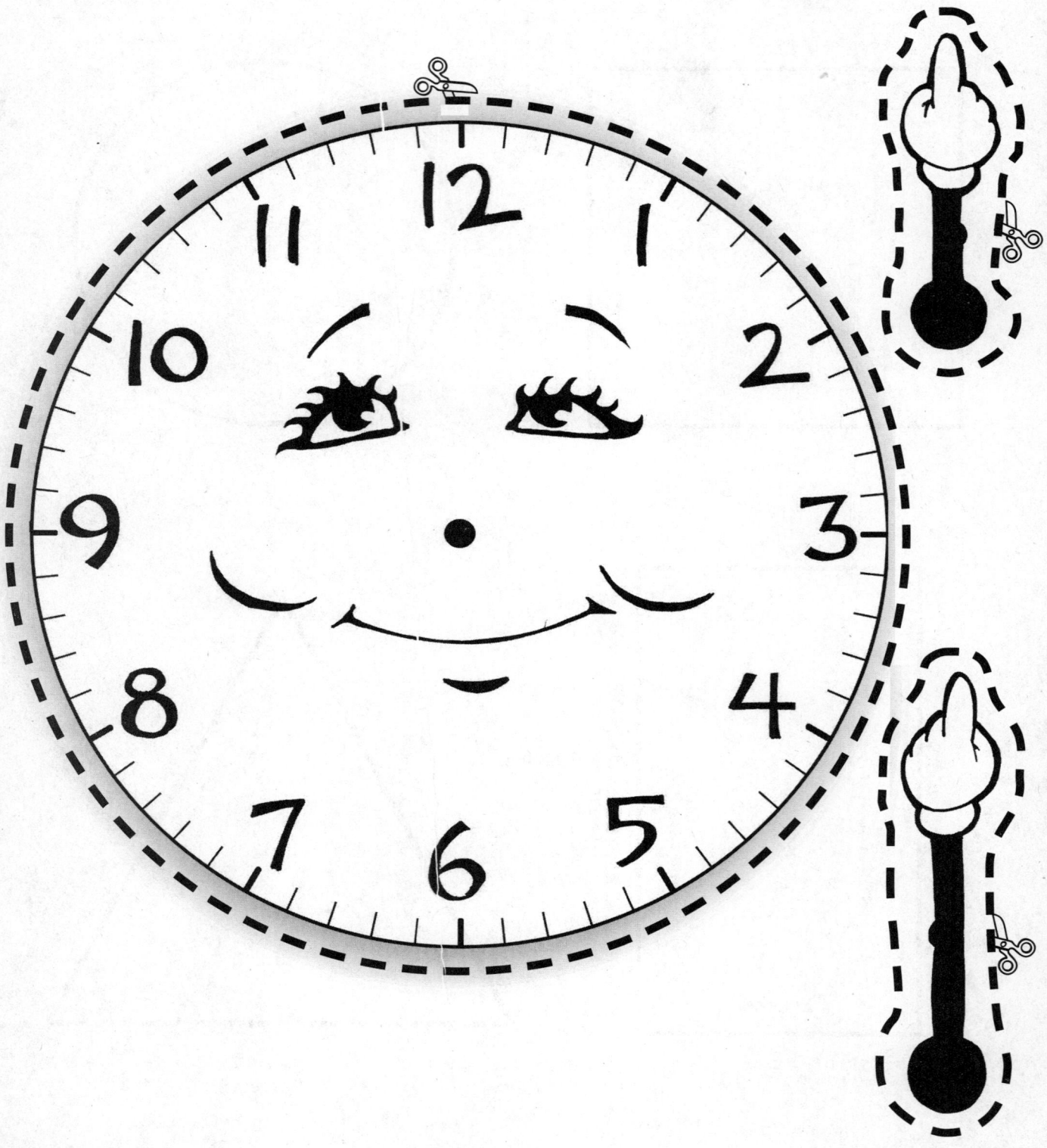

www.harcourtschoolsupply.com
© Harcourt Achieve Inc. All rights reserved.

128

Resources: Clock
Math: First Grade, SV 9937-6